Early Creedal Formulations
and Theological Discourse:

Toward a Systematic Understanding
of Theology via the Creedal Process

Early Creedal Formulations and Theological Discourse:

Toward a Systematic Understanding of Theology via the Creedal Process

Mark A. Moore

An Imprint of the
Global Center for Religious Research
1312 17th Street • Suite 549
Denver, Colorado 80202

info@gcrr.org • gcrr.org

GCRR Press
An imprint of the Global Center for Religious Research
1312 17th Street Suite 549
Denver, CO 80202
www.gcrr.org

DOI: 10.33929/GCRRPress.EarlyCreedalFormulations

Typesetting/Copyediting: Holly Lipovits

Library of Congress Cataloging-in-Publication Data

Early creedal formulations and theological discourse: toward a systematic understanding of theology via the creedal process / Mark A. Moore
p. cm.
Includes bibliographic references.
ISBN (Print): 978-0-578-78395-6
1. Creeds—History.   2. Theology, Doctrinal.   I. Title.

BR 60-67   .M667   2020

ℭℬ

To Kelli, Dylan, Beau, and all my family and friends.

Without your love and patience this project would not have happened. I can never thank you enough for all the ways that you supported me.

Contents

Acknowledgments

I would like to thank Dr. Edward Smither, Dr. Leo Percer, Dr. Kenneth Cleaver, and the rest of the faculty of the Rawlings School of Divinity at Liberty University. Throughout the process of writing this, Dr. Smither was an excellent mentor and greatly enhanced the finished product with his thoughtful guidance.

I would like to thank the faculty and staff of William Jessup University for their support and encouragement. Many conversations over coffee were had in the process of this research, and I cherish each one of them and the influence they had on my work. I am also grateful for the many students of theology whom I have had the pleasure of teaching over the last decade and the role that each has played in my own theological development.

I would like to thank the pastoral staff and congregation at Faith Legacy Church for their encouragement and support of my family. I would also like to thank my parents, John and Rebecca Moore, for their love and support throughout my long educational career.

Finally, I would like to thank my wife, Kelli, for her sacrifice and grace while my nose was often stuck in a book or in front of a screen. Without her, this project could not have happened.

Introduction

Theology is a grand conversation, a dialogue with past voices and past ideas as well as a future ones. It is an open dialogue in which one may explore the depths and intricacies of God but it is also a structured dialogue, guided by God's own revelation in the Living Word and the Holy Scriptures. One has the freedom to explore the inexhaustible arena of theology, but not the freedom to assert whatever one wishes to be true about God while remaining faithful to the nature of God and God's interaction with the world as revealed through Jesus and Scripture. The grand dialogue of Christian theology is defined by certain essential identity markers, primary affirmations of the Christian story of God, which serve to give Christian theology its unique identity. Since the time of the Incarnation and the formation of the new community of God, the church has been identifying and attempting to articulate these essential identity markers, many of which are summarized and captured in the early creedal formulations of the Christian community.

These early creedal formulations, whether found in the New Testament itself or hammered out in later church councils, defined the essential claims of what Christians believed about God. In this way these early creedal statements stood as essential identity markers for Christian theology which guided the greater theological conversation. They were not intended to give final answers for the great questions about God, in effect ending the conversation. Rather, they were intended to guide the grand theological discourse of the church into a faithful articulation of the revelation of God.

John Howard Yoder notes that the creeds served as fenceposts defining the basic tenets of Christianity as found in Scripture. Yoder writes that the creeds are part of "the history to which God has chosen to lead his confused people toward perhaps at least a degree of understanding of certain dangers, certain things not to say if we are to remain faithful." Stanley Hauerwas suggests that Yoder is making the point that the "use of the creeds sets parameters beyond which faithful readings of Scripture will be unlikely."

Tertullian, writing on the Rule of Faith, which serves as a sort of protocreed during the early apostolic period, notes, "Provided the essence of the Rule is not disturbed, you may seek and discuss as much as you like. You may give full rein to your itching curiosity where any point seems unsettled and ambiguous or dark and obscure." Here Tertullian highlights the vast freedom enjoyed within the parameters of the Rule. For Tertullian, the Rule did not serve as the final answer for all theological investigation but rather its proper measuring rod. Augustine defines the purpose of the creeds as nourishment for young believers:

> The purpose of which [compilation] was, that individuals who are but beginners and sucklings among those who have been born again in Christ, and who have not yet been strengthened by most diligent and spiritual handling and understanding of the divine Scriptures, should be furnished with a summary, expressed in few words, of those matters of necessary belief which were subsequently to be explained to them in many words, as they made progress and rose to [the height of] divine doctrine, on the assured and steadfast basis of humility and charity.

Here Augustine notes that the creeds are summaries of the key elements of the Christian faith that should lead to more discussion and explanation as the person spiritually matures.

Karl Barth also stresses the guiding factor of early creeds and confessions of the church in terms of theological discourse. For Barth, the creeds order theological discourse and keep it faithful to the revelation of God in Jesus Christ. In his work *Credo*, an examination of the theology of the Apostles' Creed, Barth asserts, "Instead of calling to order, Dogmatics has to be called to order and corrected by the church's proclamation that has kept to better ways."[1]

Michael Bird, in his work *What Christians Ought to Believe*, stresses the importance of creedal statements in shaping and directing theological discourse as well. He states that in creeds, "you are saying: this is the stuff that really matters. You are declaring: this is where the boundaries of the faith need to be drawn. You are suggesting: this is what brings us together in one faith."[2] Bird especially reemphasizes the importance of creeds for certain anti-creed strands of evangelicalism, noting that creeds are first and foremost biblical and carry on biblical traditions as well as defend the faith from heretical views.

---

[1] Karl Barth, *Credo* (New York: Charles Scribner's Sons, 1962), 6. Throughout Barth uses the term dogmatics to refer to work of systematic theology.

[2] Michael F. Bird, *What Christians Ought to Believe: An Introduction to Christian Doctrine through the Apostles' Creed*, Kindle ed. (Grand Rapids, MI: Zondervan, 2016), 18.

While theology is a grand conversation, it is also a series of smaller conversations, side discussions of specific doctrines. These smaller conversations are narrower in scope than the broad categories summarized in the creeds and explore the various subcategories of theology. While these smaller conversations are free and exploratory, they are also in need of guidance, guidance offered by the creedal process.

In this book, we will examine the function of early creedal formulations as essential identity markers in theological discourse with the goal of constructing an approach to the various subcategories of systematic theology that mirrors the creedal process. This approach, which I have termed the Essential Identity Markers model or simply EIM, seeks to identify and articulate the essential identity markers of a given theological subcategory, in order to define the proper parameters for theological discourse while still allowing such discourse to develop and expand within the articulated identity markers.

The Need for the Study

Nearly two millennia of Christian theology have given rise to numerous theological voices. In many ways, though, these voices have become too numerous and often appear contradictory. Augustine held a particular view of theology while Luther held another. Wesley opposed Calvin. Barth eluded both liberal and conservative viewpoints in some areas. While these voices have enriched the church's understanding of certain complexities of Christian theology, they have the potential of leaving the average student of theology or layperson in a haze of confusion, wondering what exactly Christians believe about anything. This confusion has led to what may be considered a form of Christian agnosticism. Many theological classes have become surveys of historical voices which often leave students questioning if anything can be truly known about theology.

The time has come to reinforce the essential claims of Christian theology, to define the parameters once again. The creedal process of identifying and articulating the essential claims of Christian theology serves as a guide for the EIM method of identifying and articulating the essential identity markers of each subcategory of theology. Following the creedal process in the EIM model allows the church to enter the grand conversation again and again from a place of agreement, a place of shared, common belief.

The EIM model can guide each new generation as it attempts to understand the handed-down proclamations of the church while also breaking new ground. Barth stressed the vital importance of holding theology and the creeds in dialogue for just this purpose: "Because the Church must again and again understand its Confession anew and because it is again and again confronted with the necessity of confessing anew, it requires Dogmatics alongside the Confession."[3] Each new generation should therefore engage in theological discourse that is guided by the essential identity markers of the Christian faith and yet be free to explore the vast area within.

Research Focus

The main focus of this book will examine how the creedal process of identifying and articulating essential identity markers of the Christian faith provides a model for approaching theology that properly defines these essential identity markers for any given category while also providing sufficient space for deeper theological discourse. Some sub questions that naturally arise from this research question are as follows:

1. What is the creedal process?
2. What factors influenced the formation of early creedal statements?
3. How did the early church leaders view the function of these statements?
4. How do essential identity markers influence theological discourse?
5. How does the creedal process influence teaching theology today?

Scope and Limitations

As this book examines the creedal process, it will focus its attention only on early creedal statements. These early creedal statements will include early creedal statements found in the New Testament, the Apostles' Creed, and the Nicene Creed.[4] Later creeds or denominational-specific confessions will not be examined.

Though the creedal process carries on throughout these later creeds and confessions, these earlier creeds highlight the church's attempt to succinctly yet sufficiently define the essential identity markers of Christian theology during the earliest stages of theological discourse. These creeds and creed-like statements emerged in a setting where definition was imperative. As this book will note in the next chapter, the early creedal process was

---

[3] Barth, *Credo*, 4.

[4] In this book, the Nicene Creed will refer to the more complete Niceno-Constantinopolitan Creed of AD 381. Further research in this book will examine the full development of the Nicene Creed and will note the addition of the *et filoque* clause at the Council of Toledo in 589. Leo's Tome and the Chalcedonian Creed are also clear examples of the function of creedal formulations as essential identity markers but have been excluded from this book to focus in on the creedal process of the first three centuries of the church.

shaped by an era of multiple voices and contradictory statements about the essential tenets of this new Christian faith. It was imperative for the early church fathers to clearly define just what Christian theology, or more importantly what Christian Scripture, was saying about the essential beliefs of Christianity.

This book is limited to these early creeds and creed-like statements because they possess the most unity in terms of support from the universal church. While there were battles and schisms even with these early creeds, they have emerged from history as excellent representations of the essential elements of traditional Christian thought. The Nicene Creed, in particular, is seen as the most unifying creed, as both the East and the West have cherished it and used it in liturgical services since its formation.[5]

While this book will focus on these early creeds and creedal statements, it will not attempt to assess the essential nature of each tenet of the creeds. Rather the focus will remain on the creedal process overall. It will attempt to fully define and examine the process that shaped the formation of the creeds as well as the function of the creeds themselves in theological discourse in order to assess if this process can provide an overarching approach to systematic theology.

Defining Key Terms

Creed

Based on the Latin word *credo* which means "I believe," the term *creed* in this book will refer to a formulaic summary of essential beliefs, crafted and adopted as authoritative by the church. According to Philip Schaff, a creed is a "confession of faith for public use, or a form setting forth with authority certain articles of belief, which are regarded by the framers as necessary for salvation, or at least for the well-being of the Christian Church."[6]

The key words to note in this definition are *form* and *authority*. Creedal historian J. N. D. Kelly notes that a creed is "a fixed formula summarizing the essential articles of their religion and enjoying the sanction of ecclesiastical authority."[7] A creed has a certain form that identifies itself as a creed. This form also aids in summarizing the essential beliefs for the church to commit to memory. Creeds that have influenced theological discourse also carry with them the authority to do so.

---

[5] Edgar C. S. Gibson, *The Three Creeds* (London: Longmans, Green &, 1912), 32.

[6] Philip Schaff, *The Creeds of Christendom: With a History and Critical Notes* (Grand Rapids, MI: Baker Books, 1996), 1:4.

[7] J. N. D. Kelly, *Early Christian Creeds*, 2nd ed. (New York: D. McKay, 1961), 1.

Protocreed

The term protocreed will refer to shorter statements that function creeds but lack the scope and development of a formal creed. Many times, this term will be in reference to sayings in the New Testament that are usually short references to belief statements, whether originating with the New Testament writer or already in use by the early church.

Rule of Faith

This term was often used by the Ante-Nicene Fathers, like Irenaeus and Tertullian, to refer to the basic beliefs of the Christian faith that were handed down by the apostles. In many ways this Rule of Faith, or regula fidei, shaped the creedal process and contained the essential belief statements seen in the later formal creeds. This Rule of Faith stands as a bridge between the apostolic teaching and the creeds and canon.

Symbol

The term symbol was also used by the early church fathers in reference to the essential beliefs of the Christian faith. The term essentially means "mark" or "watchword" and highlights its function as a test for proper Christian belief.   Schaff and Badcock agree that it can be used interchangeably with the term creed, as both serve the function of a test of orthodoxy.

Essential Identity Markers

The term essential identity markers or EIMs will be used to refer to primary affirmations of the biblical narrative. These EIMs are identified and articulated by the church through the process of theological inquiry. It is an assertion of this book that the creedal process was a process of identifying and articulating these EIMs. EIMs are what make Christian theology uniquely Christian. EIM will also be used to denote the model of approaching theology mirroring the creedal process developed in this book.

A Brief Overview of Literature

The multitude of books surrounding the topic of the creeds of Christianity can be put in to two categories: (1) historical surveys and (2) theologies of the creeds themselves. This literature review will survey several works relevant to this study by dividing them into these categories. Since this study covers the influence of these early Christian creeds on theological discourse, it will also survey a third category of books that deal specifically with the topic of theological method and the purpose and function of theology. This review will begin with the historical surveys of the Christian creeds to provide an overview of the historical context of the creedal process.

Historical Surveys and Collections

In the late nineteenth century, Philip Schaff set out to provide a "symbolic library" that contained the creeds and confessions of the range of Christian denominations. The result was a robust four-volume set that stands as the most comprehensive collection of the creeds and confessions of Christendom.[8]

Particular to this study will be *Volume I – The History of the Creeds of Christendom*. In this first volume, Schaff begins by generally examining the definition and origins of creeds and then moves to more detailed studies of particular creeds beginning with the Apostles' Creed and covering all the way to the confessions of modern evangelical denominations.[9] For Schaff, the creeds and confessions of the church are "milestones and fingerboards in the history of Christian doctrine."[10] They represent the beliefs of each generation and the results of theological debates. This impressive collection is an extremely valuable resource for creedal studies.

In 1912, Edgar C. S. Gibson, the Lord Bishop of Gloucester, published an insightful, short work on what he considered the three core creeds of early Christendom: the Apostles' Creed, the Nicene Creed, and the Athanasian Creed.[11] For Gibson, similar to Schaff, these creeds emerged from the desire for faith to be expressed.[12] Gibson cites two reasons for the developments of the creed: 1) the need for "clearness and precision" in presenting the specific beliefs of the church and 2) the rise of false teaching.[13]

In 1930, F. J. Badcock sought to publish an updated work on creedal studies, especially on the origin of the Apostles' Creed. Badcock, agreeing with Harnack, argued that the creed could not be traced back to the second century as others proposed, but rather emerges in its familiar form in

---

[8] All references to Schaff's work will come from Philip Schaff, *The Creeds of Christendom: With a History and Critical Notes*, vols. I–IV (Grand Rapids, MI: Baker Books, 1996).

[9] Modern here means up to the close of 1876.

[10] Schaff, *The Creeds of Christendom*, vol. I, 4.

[11] Gibson's focus on these three creeds highlights the importance of the creedal process that occurred I the first four centuries of the Christian faith.

[12] Gibson, *The Three Creeds*, 3. See also Schaff, *The Creeds of Christendom*, vol. I, 5.

[13] Gibson, *Three* Creeds, 27.

the fourth century.[14] Here Badcock separates the content from the earlier Rule of Faith and contemporary forms of the creed. One of the main contributions of Badcock's work is his detailed descriptions of the various types of creeds and confessions, a point that has been referenced in this work already.

In January 1935, Alan Richardson published a short introduction examining the early development of Christian creeds that exerted a great deal of influence on creedal studies up to the last part of the twentieth century.[15] Richardson's appeal was offering a scholarly work that was accessible. Richardson connects the formation of the early Christian creeds with the historical experiences of the first disciples and the risen Jesus. For Richardson, Christian doctrine emerged as a way to explain these mysterious experiences.[16] In this work, Richardson traces the historical development of several key doctrines of the Christian tradition: the Trinity, the person of Christ, the Atonement, and the Holy Spirit.

In 1950, J. N. D. Kelly published what has emerged as the seminal work of the twentieth century in creedal studies. This work, which represents over a decade of work Kelly did while part of the Faculty of Theology and Religion at Oxford, surveys both the historical context of the creeds and the theology contained within the creeds.[17] Kelly surveys creedal elements in the New Testament up to the later renditions of the Apostles' Creed. Kelly's work still stands as the most authoritative work on these early creeds.

In 1960, Paul T. Fuhrman sought to reexamine the history and importance of the creeds, noting that the use of the creeds had slipped into mere formalism for many church denominations.[18] Fuhrman purposed to introduce the "principal creeds," which the church had used throughout history to state and reaffirm its core beliefs.[19] For Fuhrman, the creeds were not merely statements of belief but also acts of worship, of giving credit to a specific God: "When the early Christian said, *Credo in unum Deum*, he meant not so much, 'I believe that a God exists,' as, 'I trust in one God in

---

[14] Badcock, *The History of the Creeds*, 2–4. See also Adolf Von Harnack, *The Apostles' Creed*, trans. Stewart Means, ed. T. Bailey Saunders (London: A. and C. Black, 1901). Badcock disagreed, though, with Harnack's view that the creeds were irrelevant to Christian practice.

[15] Alan Richardson, *Creeds in the Making: A Short Introduction to the History of Christian Doctrine* (Philadelphia, PA: Fortress Press, 1981).

[16] Richardson, *Creeds in the Making*, 25.

[17] Kelly, *Early Christian Creeds*, v.

[18] This point is drawn out from the preface written by Fuhrman's colleague at Columbia Theological Seminary, Thomas H. McDill. See also Fuhrmann, *An Introduction*, 9.

[19] Fuhrman, *Creeds of the Church*, 11.

contrast to the many gods of paganism.'"[20] This connection to worship is a valuable piece in understanding the function and purpose of the early creeds.

Another compilation of the existing creeds from the New Testament to the twentieth century was edited and published by John H. Leith in 1963.[21] This compilation is more comprehensive in scope than Kelly's work and is contained in a more accessible one volume compared to Schaff's four-volume set. Leith focused on officially recognized creeds and confessions of church history but also sought to expose the reader to more obscure creeds. Leith notes that Christianity has always relied on creeds to express its beliefs because as a religion Christianity is driven by its theology.[22] Here Leith underscores the interplay of the creedal process and theology, which serves as a foundational element of this study.

In 1963, Vernon H. Neufeld added to the field of creedal studies by closely examining the earliest of the Christian confessions found in the New Testament.[23] Neufeld traces the *homologia* of early Christian tradition as it emerged from Judaism.[24] Neufeld's dissertation, from which this work is drawn, was chaired by Bruce M. Metzger and awarded a special prize by the Christian Research Foundation in 1960.

The relative boom of historical creedal studies in the middle of the twentieth century was followed by relative silence for more than two decades. In 1991, nearly sixty years after Richardson's *Creeds in the Making*, Frances M. Young sought to bring the conversion up to date with changing scholarship.[25] Young appreciated the continuing influence of Richardson's work but looked to nuance it in light of current viewpoints concerning historiography. For Richardson, asserting that Christianity was a religion founded on historical facts was important in light of the antihistoricism of the nineteenth century.[26]

Young came along to note that historical facts are always wrapped in interpretation. Therefore, understanding the development of the early creeds involves interpreting their connection to the historical facts and the beliefs of the early followers of Jesus regarding their experiences. Young structures her study by looking at specific doctrines expressed in the creeds,

---

[20] Fuhrman, *Creeds of the Church*, 11.

[21] John H. Leith, *Creeds of the Churches: A Reader in Christian Doctrine, from the Bible to the Present*, 3rd ed. (Atlanta, GA: John Knox Press, 1982).

[22] Leith, *Creeds of the Churches*, 1.

[23] Vernon H. Neufeld, *The Earliest Christian Confessions* (Grand Rapids, MI: Eerdmans, 1963).

[24] Neufeld uses the term *homologia* to signify what aspects of Christian theology were held in "agreement" and professed by a majority of the church from its inception. See Neufeld, *Earliest Christian Confessions*, 13–15.

[25] Frances M. Young, *The Making of the Creeds* (London: SCM Press, 1991).

[26] See Richardson, *Creeds in the Making*, 5–10.

much like Richardson did. Young's work is a brief yet invaluable update to earlier studies of the early development of the creeds.

In 1991, the Commission on Faith and Order held a conference on the nature of faith and creeds that resulted in a collection of papers compiled and edited by S. Mark Heim.[27] The papers cover a range of creedal studies topics but center on this common idea of the church seeking a unifying statement of belief. Several articles examine various fourth-century influences on the formation of the Nicene Creed that will prove extremely helpful for this current study.

In 2001, scholar John Behr embarked on a three-volume journey tracing the formation of Christian theology. The first volume stands as the most important for this present study. In this volume, entitled *The Way to Nicaea*, Behr examines the first three centuries of Christian thought leading up to the famed council of Nicaea.[28] Behr is quick to point out that he is not insinuating by the title that the council itself is the definitive moment of Christian theology, but rather his main goal is to examine the theological discourse that occurred and shaped the council. Behr staunchly asserts that neglecting this period of development leading up to the famous creed only leads to a misunderstanding of the council and the creed itself.[29] In many ways this work bridges the gap between a historical survey of the formation of the creeds and the theology that shaped this formation.

In 2002, Liuwe Westra completed a comprehensive survey of the origin and development of the Apostles' Creed.[30] In this work, Westra focuses on early creedal formulae and how they eventually led to the seventh-century formulation of the Apostles' Creed. In agreement with Kelly, Westra views the Apostles' Creed as a fusion of earlier Christological and Trinitarian formulations that emerged in Rome around the end of the second century and into the third.[31] Westra's survey stands as an important recent work detailing the elusive history of the Apostles' Creed.

The purpose and scope of this current study do not require a detailed history of the development. Rather, by relying on these historical surveys, this study will provide some understanding of the development of

---

[27] S. Mark Heim, ed., *Faith to Creed: Ecumenical Perspectives on the Affirmation of the Apostolic Faith in the Fourth Century: Papers of the Faith to Creed Consultation, Commission on Faith and Order, NCCCUSA, October 25–27, 1989– Waltham, Massachusetts* (Grand Rapids, MI: W.B. Eerdmans for Commission on Faith and Order, National Council of the Churches of Christ in the U.S.A., 1991).

[28] John Behr, *The Way to Nicaea*, vol. 1, The Formation of Christian Theology (Crestwood, NY: St. Vladimir's Seminary Press, 2001).

[29] Behr, *The Way to Nicaea*, 6.

[30] Liuwe H. Westra, *The Apostles' Creed: Origin, History, and Some Early Commentaries* (Turnhout, Belgium: Brepols, 2002).

[31] Westra, *The Apostles' Creed: Origin, History, and Some Early Commentaries*, 21–72.

creeds with the goal of understanding how these creeds guided theological discourse. Constructing a systematic approach to theology by means of the creedal process is another goal of this study. To accomplish this, this study will attempt to show the value in identifying and articulating the essential identity markers of each category of theology as appropriate boundaries for theological discourse.

In 2003, famed historical theologian Jaroslav Pelikan published a historical and theological guide to the great creeds and confessions of the Christian tradition.[32] This expansive work covers four major categories of creedal development: general definitions of creeds and confessions, the genesis of creeds, the authority of creeds, and the history of development from the apostolic period up to modern Christianity. As a premier historical theologian Pelikan pulls together a wide array of research to build a solid understanding of creedal development. This work will prove immensely helpful for any creedal scholar.

Theology of The Creeds

The second category one notices in creedal studies is the exploration of the theology found within the specific creeds themselves. While numerous works attempt this, this section will be limited to only a handful of these types of works in order to sufficiently show the scope and range of books in this category.

In 1935, Karl Barth published an in-depth survey of the theology of the Apostles' Creed entitled *Credo* and again revisited the creed in 1958 with a commentary of the creed in light of Calvin's catechism.[33] In the earlier *Credo*, Barth works his way through each significant point of the Apostles' Creed in order to extrapolate the original meaning of the creed and also to understand it better in light of modern thought. Being influenced by Anselm, Barth firmly believed that each new generation needed to understand again the core beliefs of the Christian faith. This is the work of theology, or *dogmatics* in Barthian terminology.

For Barth these core beliefs were contained in the creed and the creed itself provided a great basis for understanding theology. He says, "The Credo is fitted to be the basis of a discussion of the chief problems of Dogmatics not only because it furnishes, as it were, a ground-plan of Dogmatics but above all because the meaning, aim and essence of Dogmatics and the meaning, aim and essence of the Credo, if they are not

---

[32] Jaroslav Pelikan, *Credo: Historical and Theological Guide to Creeds and Confessions of Faith in the Christian Tradition* (New Haven, CT: Yale University Press, 2003).

[33] See Barth, *Credo*, and *The Faith of the Church: A Commentary on the Apostles' Creed According to Calvin's Catechism* (New York: Meridian Books, 1958).

identical, yet stand in the closest connection."[34] This connection will prove helpful in laying the foundation for this study.

Cambridge professor John Burnaby examined the theology of the Nicene Creed in 1960 in his work *The Belief of Christendom*, which was the result of a series of lectures he presented to the Cambridge Divinity Faculty.[35] Burnaby notes the influence of Kelly's earlier work on the creeds and points to the Nicene Creed as the chief summary of the Christian faith.

Lectures given at Emmanuel College, Cambridge, by Hugh Burnaby (no relation to the above Burnaby) examining the theology of the Apostles' Creed were posthumously published in 1961. Both this series and the series by John Burnaby highlight the emphasis on creedal studies that emerged in the mid-twentieth century, especially in Great Britain.

As seen in the above subsection on historical surveys of the creeds, the relative interest in creedal studies was followed by a relative decline in interest, especially in the growing evangelical church. Toward the end of the twentieth century and into the twenty-first century, though, a resurgence has occurred, especially in terms of reexamining and reaffirming the theology of the earliest creeds. Many of these works were written for lay people with the intent of teaching theology. In 1991, Alister McGrath published a study focused on understanding and applying the Apostles' Creed, and in 1998, Michael Horton examined the theology of the Apostles' Creed in an attempt to reaffirm the heart of Christian faith and belief.[36]

Most recently, in 2016, Michael Bird released a similar work to Horton's, covering the essential elements of Christian belief as expressed in the Apostles' Creed under the pointed title, *What Christians Ought to Believe*.[37] Bird specifically notes the need for affirming the creedal nature of Christianity in the evangelical tradition, which during the late twentieth century became staunchly opposed to the use of creeds in the church.[38]

Bird's work stands as the most recent representative of this renewed interest in the creeds and will prove quite helpful in exploring the theology of the Apostles' Creed, yet it stands outside the main goal of this study. The goal here is to use these various explorations of the theology presented in these early creeds as a means of understanding the creedal process better, which then will be applied as a new approach to systematic theology.

---

[34] Barth, *Credo*, 1.

[35] John Burnaby, *The Belief of Christendom: A Commentary on the Nicene Creed* (London: SPCK, 1960).

[36] See Alister E. McGrath, *I Believe: Understanding and Applying the Apostles' Creed* (Grand Rapids, MI: Zondervan, 1991). See also Michael Scott Horton, *We Believe: Recovering the Essentials of the Apostles' Creed* (Nashville, TN: Word Pub., 1998).

[37] Michael F. Bird, *What Christians Ought to Believe: An Introduction to Christian Doctrine through the Apostles' Creed* (Grand Rapids, MI: Zondervan, 2016).

[38] Ibid., 17–18.

The Creedal Process and Theological Method

The third subsection of books this review will briefly survey pertains to works that either connect the creedal process with theology or ones that provide sufficient definitions of the discipline of theology in order to support the current study's focus of applying the creedal process to the process of systematic theology. In the evangelical tradition, many of the recent works stressing the connection between creeds and theology act as apologetic works stressing a renewal of interest in creeds as necessary for the church. In 2010, Robert Jensen, as a part of a series exploring the use of Scripture in the church, closely examines the connection between canon and creed. Jensen sufficiently shows that there is no struggle between creed and canon and in fact creeds are founded in Scripture and Scripture is full of creeds or creed-like formulas.

Jensen's work was followed by the work of Carl Trueman who stresses the necessity of creeds and confessions for the church and specifically the evangelical church, which includes some factions, Trueman underscores, that take pride in having no creed. While Trueman does not examine the theology of any given creed, he presents the case that a desperate need for the creedal process exists in the church today.

As stated earlier, it is important to also survey a handful of works that connect this study's research with the function and purpose of theology as a discipline. In order to apply the creedal process toward a systematic understanding of theology, examining those works that present theology in a manner influenced by the creedal process will be most important. These works and their authors will become dialogue partners of sorts for this study in terms of how they present the theological process.

Toward the end of his career, Karl Barth set out to summarize his decades of teaching and deep thinking about the topic of theology in a series of lectures he gave in the United States, which in turn compose what he has called an introductory examination of theology. This work combined with the earlier work, Credo, presents an integral understanding of the nature of theology and how the creeds give shape to the process.

Collected from decades of teaching theology, Anabaptist theologian John Howard Yoder's Preface to Theology presents theology as a historical stream guided along by various "communicators," like prophets, biblical writers, or Jesus himself. This stream carries with it the tradition of the past but also forges new ground for future generations. For Yoder, the various creeds and confessions of church history also guided this process.

In 1984, Yale theologian George Lindbeck published his groundbreaking work, The Nature of Doctrine, in which he presents an alternative approach to theology, termed the cultural-linguistic approach. In this work, Lindbeck presents church doctrines as being "communally authoritative teachings regarding beliefs and practices that are considered essential to the identity or welfare of the group in question," as well as asserting that doctrines are second-order statements that guide theological discourse.

While it is beyond the scope of this section to debate Lindbeck's reference to doctrines as second-order guidelines and not first-order affirmations, his model does present an interesting understanding of the connection between the creedal and theological process. For Lindbeck, the doctrines developed by the church were guided by "regulative principles," such as the "monotheistic principle," the "principle of historical specificity," et cetera, and these regulative principles were expressed in the creeds and helped form the emerging Christian identity.

To fully examine the function of early creedal formulations as essential identity markers in theological discourse, this book provides an overview of creedal development. The articles affirmed in the conciliar creeds have their foundation in the biblical narrative and were not mere inventions of the councils, therefore, provide an excellent model for identifying and articulating EIMS.

Three case studies will also be examined which trace the development of three subcategories of theology: (1) Trinity and Christology, (2) creation, and (3) the Atonement. These case studies focus on how creedal affirmations directed the theological discourse of the centuries leading up to the conciliar creeds of the fourth century. With each case study, a survey of seven theological voices will show how later theological discourse was further influenced by creedal affirmations as essential identity markers. The book concludes with an examination of the benefits of the EIM model. The grand conversation of theology continues and invites each of us to have a voice. The EIM model serves as a helpful companion in this process.

1

A Historical Overview of Creedal Development
(From New Testament Creedal Formulations to the Nicene Creed)

The historical development of Christian theology has shown that from its very origins Christianity has placed a high value on what a person believes. This emphasis on orthodoxy stands in contrast to more orthopraxy-oriented religions like Hinduism and Buddhism.

Frances Young even contrasts Christianity with its Judaic roots, noting that while "Christianity arose within Judaism...Judaism is not an orthodoxy, but an orthopraxy — its common core is 'right action' rather than 'right belief.'"[1] Young's argument highlights the fact that the Christian tradition has uniquely placed a high value on the need for its adherents to believe a particular thing about God. Though the creedal process finds roots in Judaism and certain Hebrew Bible passages clearly influenced the creedal development of the New Testament and the early church, one can state that Christianity is a particularly creedal religion, continually summarizing its core beliefs in short yet powerful formulations.[2]

Faced with this realization, one wonders why Christianity is particularly concerned with orthodoxy and expressing this right belief in creedal statements. As Timothy Johnson traces the historical development of the creedal process from the pages of the New Testament up to the major councils of the fourth century, he makes a critical observation. Johnson notes that for the early church, "the experience of Jesus demanded a new telling of

---

[1] See Young, *Making of the* Creeds, 1. Johnson notes that while Judaism and Islam both have an extensive law system to govern behavior, both have "allowed an astonishing freedom of conviction and intellectual expression." See Johnson, *Creed*, 9.

[2] Several other creedal scholars have noted the particular emphasis on which the Christian religion places on the development of creedal statements and the need for its adherents to believe a particular thing about the God they worship. See Leith, *Creeds of the Churches*, 1–2; Johnson, *Creed*, 9–10; Jenson, *Canon and Creed*, 14–15; Bird, *What Christians Ought to Believe*, 13.

the biblical story, and the proper understanding of that story needed to be defined and defended."[3]

Two key words from Johnson's observation not only explain the unique emphasis Christianity placed on creedal affirmations but also help uncover the purpose and function of the creeds: they *defined* and *defended*. As asserted in the initial chapter, the creeds were designed to define the great theological conversation as this new story of Jesus was being retold and passed on to new generations and new cultures. The creeds passed on the essential identity markers of the Christian story. The design of the creeds provided a defense of the new Christian story from a retelling of the story that was inconsistent with the experience of the earliest followers of Jesus. As it traces the historical development of the creedal process from New Testament creedal statements to the more formalized Apostles' Creed and Nicene Creed, this chapter will also stress the function of the creeds as defining the theological conversation and defending the true Christian story.

Before beginning to examine the various creedal statements found in the New Testament, it will be helpful to note the different types of creeds that emerged in the first four centuries of the church. Badcock notes three main types of creeds: baptismal, conciliar, and personal professions of faith.[4] While noting that baptismal creeds were used to prepare candidates for baptism, Badcock further breaks down this classification into two parts: interrogatory and declaratory.[5] Interrogative creeds were a formulated series of questions answered in the affirmative by the baptismal candidate, while declarative creeds were worded as "I believe" or "We believe" professions of faith.[6] For Badcock, conciliar creeds were crafted by church councils as tests of orthodoxy. With these distinctions in mind, Badcock associates the Apostles' Creed with the baptismal classification and the Nicene Creed with the conciliar classification.[7] Before tracing the development of these two great creeds of Christendom, the roots of creedal development in the New Testament should first be examined.

---

[3] Johnson, *Creed*, 21. Johnson also stresses the importance of understanding the creeds not as later "impositions upon the simple gospel story—as some critics charge— but rather a natural development of Christianity best understood in light of the specific character of the Christian religion and the crises it faced from the start," 10.

[4] Badcock, *History of the Creeds*, 14–15.

[5] Ibid.

[6] Kelly emphasizes here, though, that the evidence supports that only interrogative baptismal creeds can be found in early liturgies prior to the third century. Declaratory creeds based on the earlier interrogations develop later into the third century. See Kelly, *Early Christian Creeds*, 48.

[7] Badcock, *History of the Creeds*, 14–15.

New Testament Creedal Statements

The great creeds of the church did not simply appear at the turn of the fourth century; rather they emerged from a process that was in motion even before Christianity arose. In tracing the historical development of New Testament creedal statements, the Hebrew Bible origins of such statements, the structure of the statements, and the general function the statements served for the New Testament authors will be surveyed. This section will also more closely examine a few New Testament creedal statements to understand their particular function in the development of early Christian theology.

Hebrew Bible Origins

Michael Bird, in agreement with other prominent scholars,[8] traces the creedal roots of the New Testament to Deuteronomy 6:4–5, the Shema: "Hear, O Israel: The Lord is our God, the Lord alone. You shall love the Lord your God with all your heart, and with all your soul, and with all your might."[9] The Jews committed the Shema to memory and recited it daily. Bird considers the Shema the simplest confession of Israel's faith in one God and notes that it served to differentiate Judaism from the various polytheistic religions in practice at the time.[10] Neufeld considered the Shema as a summary of the "homologia" of Judaism, noting Josephus's assertion that the acknowledgement of God as one served to unify the Jews.[11] Neufeld also noted that a copy of the Shema was carried by Jewish males in their phylacteries to serve as a reminder of who the God of the Jews truly was and what God called them to do in response.

Johnson highlights three features of the Shema that will aid us in understanding the origins of the creedal process as well as the function of the creeds.[12] First, Johnson notes that the Shema calls the whole community, rather than just specific individuals, to a commitment to God. It is a communal affirmation of commitment, not simply an individual confession.

---

[8] Bird, *What Christians Ought to Believe*, 18. See also Johnson, *Creed*, 11, and Neufeld, *Earliest Christian Confessions*, 35.

[9] All quotations from Scripture will come from the New Revised Standard Version.

[10] Bird, *What Christians Ought to Believe*, 18–19.

[11] Neufeld, *Earliest Confessions*, 35, 37. See also, Josephus, *Antiquities* 5.II2. For Neufeld, *homologia* represented the essential convictions and beliefs held by a religious group. These essential beliefs were the common point of agreement for the majority within a given religious group. See 20–21.

[12] Johnson, *Creed*, 11. The remainder of this paragraph summarizes Johnson's three distinct features of the Shema in order to show how it lays a strong foundation for the function of the New Testament creeds.

Second, it is distinctly exclusive. The God of Israel, YHWH, is the one and only God and worthy of Israel's worship and allegiance. This exclusivity stands as an essential identity marker for the Jews. In a polytheistic world, they worshiped YHWH above all other gods. Lastly Johnson notes that the Shema is also a personal commitment. Each individual Israelite is called to love God with his or her whole being. In light of these three features, Johnson draws out a dual functionality for the Shema in that it "both defines the one to whom loyalty is given and defines Israel among the nations by its unique loyalty to this deity."[13]

John Leith, in his exhaustive compilation of the creeds of the church, also recognizes the latter half of 1 Kings 18:39, along with the Shema, as a declaratory affirmation of Judaism: "When all the people saw it, they fell on their faces and said, 'The Lord indeed is God; the Lord indeed is God.'"[14] While considering both the Shema and 1 Kings 18:39 declaratory affirmations, Leith also describes Deuteronomy 26:5–9 as a historical creed, retelling and summarizing the story of Israel:

> You shall make this response before the Lord your God: "A wandering Aramean was my ancestor; he went down into Egypt and lived there as an alien, few in number, and there he became a great nation, mighty and populous. When the Egyptians treated us harshly and afflicted us, by imposing hard labor on us, we cried to the Lord, the God of our ancestors; the Lord heard our voice and saw our affliction, our toil, and our oppression. The Lord brought us out of Egypt with a mighty hand and an outstretched arm, with a terrifying display of power, and with signs and wonders; and he brought us into this place and gave us this land, a land flowing with milk and honey."

Here a historical creed served the same function as the declarative creed, in that it summarized the action of God in uniquely calling and caring for the Jews.

The foundation of the New Testament creedal statements, as well as the later more formal creeds, is clearly visible in these Hebrew Bible creedal statements. The latter creeds and creedal statements serve the same function in clearly identifying the God of Christian theology as well as providing Christians with essential and unique identity markers. Johnson underscores the connection this way: "the Christian creed takes its origin in just this need to express a people's experience and story, and to distinguish their specific allegiance in the context of competing claims. It is, like the *Shema*, a call for communal, personal, and exclusive commitment."[15] Bird agrees with

---

[13] Johnson, *Creed*, 11.

[14] Leith, *Creeds of the Churches*, 14.

[15] Johnson, *Creed*, 11–12.

Johnson here, stressing that given the context of the essential claims of Judaism "the early church developed their own creeds to summarize what they believed the God of Israel *had done* and *would yet do* in the Lord Jesus Christ."[16]

The Structure of New Testament Formulations

The transition to a closer look at specific New Testament creedal formulations will require a focus on how to recognize and identify these early creedal statements within the text of the New Testament. German theologian Ethelbert Stauffer provides perhaps the most extensive list of criteria for recognizing the unique structure of New Testament creedal formulations. His twelve criteria are:

1. Often the most reliable guide is the language of the immediate context: the creedal formulae or their constitutive elements are inserted and introduced by such words as "deliver," "believe," or "confess," e.g., Rom. 10:9.

2. The presence of a creedal formula can often be detected by textual dislocations. Frequently when such a formula is inserted the context or the formula or both suffer changes, e.g., 1 Tim. 3:16.

3. Frequently the creedal formula fails to fit into the context syntactically, e.g., Rev 1:4.

4. The creedal formula often exhibits a different linguistic usage, terminology, or style from its context, e.g., 1 Cor. 16:22.

5. We can often see how quite different passages repeat the same creedal formula with very little difference in each case, e.g., 2 Cor. 5:22; 8:9.

6. Creedal formulae often strike us by their simple and clear syntax. They avoid particles, conjunctions, and complicated constructions, and prefer parataxis to hypotaxis. Their thought proceeds by thesis rather than argument, e.g., Acts 4:10.

7. Creedal formulae often stand out by reason of their monumental stylistic construction. They favor an antithetic or anaphoral style, e.g., 1 Tim. 3:16.

8. Creedal formulae are often rhythmical in form. Unlike Greek poetry, its rhythm is not determined by quantity, but by the number of stresses or even words, e.g., 1 Cor. 15:3.

9. The Creedal formulae are often arranged in lines and strophes, e.g., Col. 1:15ff.

10. Creedal formulae are often marked by their preference for appositions and noun predicates, e.g., IgnE. 7:2.

---

[16] Bird, *What Christians Ought to Believe*, 18.

11. Creedal formulae often favor participles and relative clauses, e.g., Rom. 1:3.

12. For the most part creedal formulae refer to the elementary truths and events of salvation-history as norms, e.g., IgnTr. 9:1f.[17]

With these criteria in mind it is easier to note the certain phrases and slogans that appear to jump out of the text of the New Testament. Criteria six through eleven detail the common structure of creedal formulae. They underscore that the structure of these early creedal formulae was intentionally simple, which aided memorization. Criterion twelve also serves to highlight a fundamental function of all creedal statements: the summation of elementary or essential identity markers of the Christian narrative.

Creedal scholar J. N. D. Kelly assures his readers that discovering early creedal formulations in the New Testament should not come as a surprise, given that the New Testament itself openly recognizes that a tradition had been forming since the time of Christ and was being passed on.[18] For example, Jude 3 references "the faith that was once for all entrusted to the saints." Both 1 Cor 11:23 and 15:3 stress a tradition that is being passed on by Paul.

Applying the criteria laid out by Stauffer, certain key phrases and passages from the New Testament emerge. A common slogan that appears in several key passages reflects a simple confession of Jesus as Lord or Christ, or *Kurios Iēous*.[19] One reads in 1 Cor 12:3, "Therefore I want you to understand that no one speaking by the Spirit of God ever says 'Let Jesus be cursed!' and no one can say 'Jesus is Lord' except by the Holy Spirit." Here the translation committee of the NRSV has noted the slogan with quotation marks.

Again in Rom 10:9 Paul writes "If you confess with your lips that *Jesus is Lord* and believe in your heart that God raised him from the dead, you will be saved" (emphasis added). Both Kelly and Badcock note that this simple creedal formula is also stressed in the various baptismal admonitions of the New Testament (see Acts 8:16, 19:5 1 Cor 6:11).[20] Badcock asserts that it is clear from these references that affirmation of the lordship of Jesus was a primary requirement of baptismal candidates in the New Testament.

This simple formula is then expanded on in other key passages of the New Testament that fit Stauffer's criterion and provide more insight into

---

[17] Ethelbert Stauffer, *New Testament Theology*, trans. John Marsh (New York: Macmillan, 1956), 338–39.

[18] Kelly, *Early Christian Creeds*, 1–2.

[19] In Chapters 3 and 4 of *Earliest Christian Confessions*, Cullmann argues for the priority of simple Christological formulas.

[20] Kelly, *Early Christian Creeds*, 14–15; Badcock, *History of the Creeds*, 15–16.

the Jesus tradition that was forming and being passed on during the apostolic period. Rom 1:3–4 expresses a more developed yet still tightly formed theological statement on the Jesus tradition:

> The gospel concerning his Son, who was:
> descended from David according to the flesh
> and was declared to be Son of God with power according to the spirit of holiness by resurrection from the dead,
> Jesus Christ our Lord.

Rom 8:34 provides a similar list of essential affirmations of Jesus:

> Who is to condemn?
> It is Christ Jesus, who died,
> yes, who was raised,
> who is at the right hand of God,
> who indeed intercedes for us.

In 2 Tim 2:8 one finds similar essential identity markers of the early Jesus tradition:

> Remember Jesus Christ,
> raised from the dead,
> a descendant of David
> —that is my gospel.

Kelly notes that all three of these formulations appear to serve as gospel summaries that had been drawn up to aid either catechetical training or preaching.[21] In these three as well one notes the essential nature of confessing Jesus as (1) Lord, (2) raised from the dead, and (3) a descendant of David.

First Corinthians 15:3–7

There are also other more developed creedal statements in the New Testament that deserve a closer examination. This section will examine not only their content but also the particular function they served within the theological framework of the first century. The first of note is 1 Cor 15:3–7,

> For I handed on to you as of first importance what I in turn had received:

---

[21] Kelly, *Early Christian Creeds*, 17.

that Christ died for our sins in accordance with the scriptures,
and that he was buried,
and that he was raised on the third day in accordance with the scriptures,
and that he appeared to Cephas,
then to the twelve.
Then he appeared to more than five hundred brothers and sisters at one time, most of
    whom are still alive, though some have died.
Then he appeared to James,
then to all the apostles.

In verse 3, Paul clearly notes that what is being shared is the core of the Jesus tradition that had been passed down from the earliest followers of Jesus. Neufeld stresses the "primitiveness" of this passage and highlights the notion of passing on what has been received, or *paradosis* terminology, as sufficient evidence for scholarly acceptance of this creed as pre-Pauline.[22] Stauffer considers the content of this creedal formulation a "quadripartite summary" of the narrative of the Gospel: Christ died, was buried, was raised, and appeared to his followers.[23] Kelly asserts that 1 Cor 15:3–7 is "manifestly a summary drawn up for catechetical purposes or for preaching: it gives the gist of the Christian message in concentrated form."[24]

    In agreeing with Kelly that this creedal formulation represents a concentrated form of the Christian message used for training or preaching, one can draw out several essential identity markers of the earliest tradition of the Jesus story. First, the death of Christ stands as a fundamental affirmation. Without death there is no resurrection. Without resurrection there is no life. Likewise, Christ's burial reinforces that death actually occurred. Calvin, in his commentary on 1 Corinthians, notes that the reality of the death of Christ is made more vivid with the mention of his burial.[25] This is why references to burial are found in later creedal development. Irenaeus, in his attack against Gnosticism, referenced the pre-Pauline tradition of burial to reinforce the humanity of Jesus.[26] Tertullian also stressed the Pauline and pre-Pauline references to burial to counteract the teaching of the Docetists.[27]

---

    [22] Neufeld, *Earliest Christian Confessions*, 47.
    [23] Stauffer, *New Testament Theology*, 245. Neufeld stresses here that the descriptive phrases that mention who the risen Jesus appeared to were added later, by Paul, to include himself and other witnesses. See Neufeld, *Earliest Christian Confessions*, 47.
    [24] Kelly, *Early Christian Creeds*, 17.
    [25] John Calvin, *First Epistle*, 314.
    [26] Irenaeus, *Against Heresies* 3.18.3.
    [27] Tertullian, *On the Resurrection of the Flesh* 48.

Both Christ's death and burial would not be of any factor though unless the third essential identity marker is added: resurrection. The resurrection serves as the pinnacle of the gospel story. Anthony Thiselton asserts that Paul's usage of the perfect passive voice stresses the reality of the resurrection, a point Paul is emphatically making in this passage.[28] Paul then used the fourth clause concerning the appearances of the risen Jesus to reinforce the reality of the resurrection.

It could surely be said that Paul's overall purpose for using this tradition was to stress the reality of the resurrection as an essential identity marker. This purpose also aids in underscoring the general purpose of this pre-Pauline creedal formulation, mainly the identification, articulation, and, one could add, the preservation of the essential identity markers of the Christian faith.

Philippians 2:5–11

Phil 2:5–11 stands as another early Christian confession, also considered by many to possess hymn-like qualities:[29]

Let the same mind be in you that was in Christ Jesus,
  who, though he was in the form of God,
    did not regard equality with God
    as something to be exploited,
  but emptied himself,
    taking the form of a slave,
    being born in human likeness.
And being found in human form,
  he humbled himself
  and became obedient to the point of death—
  even death on a cross.

---

[28] Anthony C. Thiselton, *The First Epistle to the Corinthians: A Commentary on the Greek Text*, NIGTC (Grand Rapids, MI: W.B. Eerdmans, 2000), 1193.

[29] Richard N. Longenecker, *New Wine into Fresh Wineskins: Contextualizing the Early Christian Confessions* (Peabody, MA: Hendrickson Publishers, 1999), 12. Gordon Fee stands out as a noticeable exception to scholarly consensus on Phil 2:5–11 constituting a pre-Pauline hymn. See Gordon D. Fee, "Philippians 2:5–11: Hymn or Exalted Pauline Prose?," *Bulletin for Biblical Research* 2 (1992). Fee argues that while this passage possesses several of the criteria for labeling it as a hymn it should not be thought of as pre-Pauline for it fits the flow of Paul's argumentation in the passage too well. At the very least, Fee concludes that this passage, if it has any prior tradition, is thoroughly taken over by Paul in language and composition. It is not our purpose in this book to "prove" the pre-Pauline status of this passage so we will not take up an effort to engage with Fee on this matter. Rather we will side with the majority of scholars who trace a heavy pre-Pauline tradition here.

> Therefore God also highly exalted him
> and gave him the name
> that is above every name,
> so that at the name of Jesus
> every knee should bend,
> in heaven and on earth and under the earth,
>   and every tongue should confess
> that Jesus Christ is Lord,
> to the glory of God the Father

This passage, again, speaks to the very nature of Christ, summarizing the fundamental or essential elements of the Christian understanding of Jesus. In way of summarizing the main points of the early Christian tradition, it is worth noting that the hymn-like qualities seen in this passage give it a different function than that of the creedal statements examined above. Worship also appears to be a function of this creedal passage, a declaration of who Jesus really is and why he is worthy of praise.[30]

Conclusion

With the addition of worship as a function of early New Testament creedal formulations, it is clear in this brief survey that these early creedal formulations served several functions. The primary function does stand out though as a simple affirmation of the essential identity markers of the Christian story. They served as the means of passing on this great tradition in a way that naturally flowed from one person to another.

Apostles' Creed

Historical Development

Once embarked upon, tracing the history of the Apostles' Creed proves to be an arduous and complicated task. The first appearances of the Apostles' Creed in its current form date to the eighth century with the final Latin formula, known as the *Textus Receptus*, dating even later, to the sixteenth century.[31] Given these late dates, Gibson notes that the Apostles' Creed could be considered the latest of the core creeds of early Christendom, yet as Gibson and others also note, it undoubtedly bears a connection with creedal

---

[30] In his collection of early Christian creeds, Leith lists Phil 2:5–11 as a "liturgical confession." See Leith, *Creeds of the Churches*, 15.

[31] See Kelly, *Early Christian Creeds,* 369. See also Piotr Ashwin-Siejkowski, *The Apostles' Creed: The Apostles' Creed and Its Early Christian Context* (London: T & T Clark, 2009), 4.

formulations of an early time, resembling some of the earliest Christian confessions of the Western church.[32] It is simultaneously a representation of the later development of the creedal process and one of the earliest expressions of the church.

While the theory that the Apostles' Creed can be traced back to the original Apostles has been thoroughly rejected, a great number of scholars draw a connection between the current Apostles' Creed and the baptismal formulation known as the Old Roman Symbol.[33] Jensen asserts that to accept the Apostles' Creed as only an eighth century or later creation of the church would be a failure to recognize its theological and creedal development.[34] The Apostles' Creed did not simply appear in the eighth century, but the line tracing its development from the Old Roman Symbol is not straight and often blurred. It is the task of this section to reflect briefly upon this creedal development from baptismal symbol to established creed.

To do so, this section will start with the later, most complete appearances of the Apostles' Creed and work back to the Old Roman Symbol. Once the historical development is briefly traced, the function of the Apostles' Creed throughout this time will be highlighted.

The final Latin formulation of the Apostles' Creed, the exact form that is still used today, is drawn from the writings of Melchior Hittorp, the canon of Cologne, published in 1568.[35] Kelly notes that this final Latin formulation is the exact form that was viewed as authoritative by the church in the West throughout the later Middle Ages and adopted by the reformers.[36] The text of this final formulation reads as follows:

I believe in God the Father almighty,
creator of heaven and earth;
I believe in Jesus Christ, His only Son, our Lord,
Who was conceived by the Holy Spirit, born of the Virgin Mary,
Suffered under Pontius Pilate, was crucified dead and buried,

---

[32] Gibson, *Three Creeds*, 39.

[33] See Kelly, *Early Christian Creeds*, 398; Badcock, *History of the Creeds*, 9; Johnson, *Creed*, 30; Furhman, *Great Creeds*, 27; Ashwin-Siejkowski, *The Apostles' Creed*, 4; Gibson, *Three Creeds*, 39; Harnack, *The Apostles' Creed*, 40; Jensen, *Canon and Creed*, 43. See also Arthur McGiffert Cushman, *The Apostles' Creed: Its Origin, Its Purpose, and Its Historical Interpretation* (New York: C. Scribner's, 1902). It is worth noting here that Badcock emphasizes that the line between the Old Roman Symbol and the Apostles' Creed is very blurred and certainty is unattainable. He sharply disagrees with Harnack who proposes to draw a clear connection between the Symbol and the Apostles' Creed.

[34] Jensen, *Canon and Creed*, 40. Jensen further suggests that even to consider it a fourth century formulation of the church does not give credit the developmental history as traced by the Old Roman Symbol.

[35] Kelly, *Early Christian Creeds*, 369.

[36] Ibid.

He descended into hell, the third day he rose again from the dead;
He ascended into heaven and sits at the right hand of God the Father almighty;
from thence he will judge the living and the dead;
I believe in the Holy Spirit,
the holy Catholic Church,
the communion of saints,
the remission of sins,
the resurrection of the flesh,
and eternal life. Amen.[37]

This final formulation represents the full and complete development of the Apostles' Creed, but little about the true origin of the creed can be known by this final form. This text will be used, though, as a starting point to then work backward toward earlier formulations of the initial centuries of Christianity.

While this sixteenth-century version represents the complete and final Latin formulation of the text, the first fully developed version of the Apostles' Creed to be comparably representative of its current form appears in the eighth century in the writings of Saint Priminius, particularly his missionary manual, *de Singulis Libris Canonicis Scarapsus*. Saint Priminius was the founder and first abbot of the monastery of Reichenau and later the abbot of the monastery at Hornbach.[38] In his writings, Priminius referenced the Apostles' Creed in terms of reminding his readers of their baptism experience and the liturgy used. In this exchange between the priest and the baptismal candidate, one sees the clear outline of the Apostles' Creed:

You were also asked by the priest, "Do you believe in God the Father almighty, creator of heaven and earth?" You replied, "I believe." And again, "Do you believe in Jesus Christ, His only Son, our Lord, Who was conceived by the Holy Spirit, born from the Virgin Mary, suffered under Pontius Pilate, was crucified, dead and buried, descended into hell, on the third day rose again from the dead, ascended to heaven, sat at the right hand of God the Father almighty, thence He will come to judge to living and the dead?" And you replied, "I believe." And the priest asked a third time, "Do you also believe in the Holy Spirit, the holy Catholic Church, the communion of saints, the remission of sins, the resurrection of the flesh, eternal life?" Either you or your god-father for you replied, "I believe."[39]

---

[37] This text is drawn from Kelly, *Early Christian Creeds*, 369. C.f. Schaff, *The Creeds of Christendom*, 21.

[38] Kelly, *Early Christian Creeds*, 398–99.

[39] This text is quoted in Kelly, *Early Christian Creeds*, 399–400.

While this reference gives us the Apostles' Creed in its final recognized form, it clearly hints at a prior formulation and prior use. Priminius does not take credit for the formation of the interrogatory sequence he depicts, which indicates that this practice clearly precedes his writing and one could assert the eighth century as well. The clear baptismal function represented here underscores one of the main functions of the Apostles' Creed, which will be highlighted after tracing more of the historical development, and also connects with the function of earlier creedal formulae that will be examined next.

When dealing with both the sixteenth- and eighth-century formulations of the Apostles' Creed, Kelly clearly notes a connection to what is known as the Old Roman Symbol.[40] Liuwe Westra reaffirms Kelly's theory and traces the roots of the Apostles' Creed back to the second century as a formulation of the Roman church.[41] While it is outside of the scope of this chapter to provide an exhaustive outline of the historical development of the Apostles' Creed from its roots in the Old Roman Symbol, it will trace a few of the steps that take us back to its initial origin.

The fourth century serves as a bridge between the Old Roman Symbol and the Apostles' Creed, particularly the writings of Rufinus (c. AD 390) and Marcellus (AD 336–341). It is also in the fourth century when one first sees the linguistic combination of symbol and apostle, *Symbolum Apostolorum*, written in a letter from the council of Milan to Pope Siricius, most likely composed by Saint Ambrose.[42]

In examining these three references to the Old Roman Symbol, it is clear that the belief that this tradition can be traced back to the original twelve apostles was alive and well. Rufinus provided a detailed narrative as to how this tradition was passed down from the apostolic period, but again this theory has been thoroughly rejected by modern scholarship for good and evident reasons.[43] The text of the Old Roman Symbol from Rufinus does prove helpful in tracing the origins of the creed. In his commentary on the

---

[40] Kelly, *Early Christian Creeds*, 369.

[41] Westra, *The Apostles' Creed*, 72. Both Kelly and Westra reject Harnack's theory that the Apostles' Creed in its final form can be traced back to the fifth century at its earliest. The similarities that will be shown between the Old Roman Symbol and the Apostles' Creed will make it clear why Kelly and Westra, along with most of the recent creedal scholarship, have rejected Harnack's assertion.

[42] Kelly, *Early Christian Creeds*, 106. Also see Ambrose, Letter 42.5, from Migne, *Patrologiae Latinae Cursus Completus,* 16, 1125.

[43] Schaff notes the following reasons for rejecting such a narrative: 1) the intrinsic improbability of the narrative, 2) the surprising silence of the New Testament writers as to the formation of such a creed, 3) the silence of the Ante-Nicene Fathers, 4) the several variations of the early rule of faith, and 5) the fact that the creed has never been recognized by the church in the East. See Schaff, *The Creeds of Christendom*, 23.

creed, what Rufinus noted as the Old Roman Symbol can be reconstructed as follows:

> I believe in God the Father almighty.
> And in Jesus Christ, his only Son, our Lord;
> Who was born by the Holy Spirit of the Virgin Mary;
> Was crucified under Pontius Pilate and was buried;
> The third day he rose from the dead;
> He ascended into heaven; and sits on the right hand of the Father;
> From thence he will come to judge the quick and the dead.
> And in the Holy Spirit,
> The Holy Church,
> the remission of sins,
> the resurrection of the flesh.[44]

Compared with the *Textus Receptus* above, the modifications are minimal but evident. Marcellus, the bishop of Ancyra in Cappadocia recorded a similar version of the symbol in Greek some sixty years before Rufinus, showing that this pattern was well-established before Rufinus.

The basic structure for the Old Roman Symbol can be traced back even further when one notes the similarities between Rufinus's version and the interrogatory baptismal creed found in the work *Apostolic Tradition* by Hippolytus dating in the early third century (c. AD 215) and written in Greek. The creed found in Hippolytus's work poses a series of questions to the baptismal candidate and is as follows:

> Do you believe in God, the Father Almighty?
> Do you believe in Christ Jesus, Son of God,
> Who was born by the Holy Spirit out of Mary the Virgin, and was crucified under Pontius Pilate and died and was buried, and rose on the third day alive from among the dead, and ascended into heaven, and sits at the right hand of the Father, to come to judge the living and the dead?
> Do you believe in the Holy Spirit, and the holy Church, and the resurrection of the flesh?[45]

Kelly notes that while the exact relation between this creed and the Old Roman Symbol is unclear, the similarities are striking and display some sort of connection.[46] Kelly goes on to assert that it is safe to say that a creed

---

[44] Text is drawn from Schaff, *The Creeds of Christendom*, 21–22. See also Kelly, *Early Christian Creeds*, 102.

[45] Text is drawn from Johnson, *Creed*, 31. See also Fuhrmann, *Great Creeds of the Church*, 27.

[46] Kelly, *Early Christian Creeds*, 107.

"remarkably like" the Old Roman Symbol was used in Rome in the third century.[47] One is also struck by the similarities with the later eighth-century version of the Apostles' Creed, making it easy to note some form of relation as well.

When tracing the historical and theological development of the Apostles' Creed from its foundation in the Old Roman Symbol, it is also important to note prior theological and creedal developments leading up to the Symbol itself. The main bridge between the apostolic kerygma found in the New Testament and the Old Roman Symbol is the Rule of Faith. The Rule of Faith represents the core of the early Patristic tradition and teachings. Bryan Litfin defines the Rule of Faith as "a confessional formula (fixed neither in wording nor in content, yet following the same general pattern) that summarized orthodox beliefs about the actions of God and Christ in the world."[48]

Paul Hartog defines it as "a concise statement of early Christian public preaching and communal belief, a normative compendium of the *kerygma*."[49] Hartog notes that the Rule of Faith was not viewed as a competitor with Scripture but was rather drawn from and founded on the biblical message.[50] Litfin observes that the Rule was initially used as a catechetical summary for baptismal preparation but was always viewed as "a convenient summary of catholic orthodoxy."[51]

Among three conclusions that Litfin makes regarding the Patristic understanding of the Rule of Faith, he notes that the Rule was used to emphasize "unchanging, absolute truths" regarding the primary affirmations of Scripture.[52] Litfin notes nine unchanging truths of the Christian faith affirmed in the various iterations of the Rule with all focusing on the action of God and the work of Jesus:

1. The act of Creation by the Father God
2. The act of Prediction through the Spirit in the Old Testament
3. The act of Incarnation by the Holy Spirit through the Virgin Mary

---

[47] Kelly, *Early Christian Creeds*, 107. Westra reaffirms this assertion in his own work, *The Apostles' Creed*, 72.

[48] Bryan Litfin, "Learning from Patristic Use of the Rule of Faith," in *The Contemporary Church and the Early Church: Case Studies in Ressourcemented*, ed. Paul A. Hartog (Eugene, OR: Pickwick Publications, 2010), under "2182."

[49] Paul Hartog, "The 'Rule of Faith' and Patristic Biblical Exegesis," *Trinity Journal* 28, no. 1 (2007): 65–66.

[50] Hartog, "The 'Rule of Faith' and Patristic Biblical Exegesis," 67. See also Litfin, "Learning," under "2462."

[51] Litfin, "Learning," under "2182."

[52] Ibid.

4. The act of Ministration in which Christ serves the world, preaches, and works miracles 5. The act of Crucifixion for the purpose of salvation

6. The act of Resurrection in triumph

7. The act of Ascension to the Father's right hand

8. The act of Proclamation by the Spirit's power in the apostolic church

9. The act of Consummation in which the dead will be raised by Christ for final judgment[53]

While no one fixed Rule of Faith exists from this period, one can piece together the core message of the Rule and note its foundational role in the development of the Old Roman Symbol. Two main Patristic writers who utilized the Rule in argumentation and theological development are Irenaeus of Lyons and Tertullian. In fact, Litfin asserts that a complete Rule of Faith does not appear before Irenaeus, though he cites traces of it in the writings of Ignatius of Antioch, Aristides of Athens, and Justin Martyr.[54] Hartog notes that Irenaeus identified the Rule with the overarching narrative of Scripture and considered it the logic of Scripture, while Tertullian also understood the Rule as the reason or order of Scripture.[55]

John Behr summarizes the content of the Rule as seen in the writings of Irenaeus as: "the one God and Father; the one Lord, the crucified and risen Jesus Christ; and the one Holy Spirit."[56] Litfin notes that in *Prescription Against Heretics*, Tertullian touched on every classic element that comprises the culmination of the Rule: "God the Creator; the Word who was born of Mary, lived, died, rose again, and ascended to heaven; the Holy Spirit who guides the church; and the promise of Christ's return for resurrection, judgment, and rewards."[57] Litfin asserts that for Tertullian and Irenaeus these elements together form the greater Christian metanarrative.[58]

In contrast with the later, formal conciliar creeds, the Rule of Faith displays a more fluid development that varies in terms of wording and nuance yet is still guided by a solidifying core. This core revolves around the tripartite confession of Father, Son, and Holy Spirit, which serves as the skeletal framework of the Old Roman Symbol. The development of the Rule and its usage in argumentation and biblical exegesis also clearly displays the long line of theological development that occurred well before the formal councils of the fourth century. The roots of the Apostles' Creed in its current

---

[53] Litfin, "Learning," under "2472."

[54] Ibid., under "2196."

[55] Hartog, "The 'Rule of Faith,'" 67.

[56] John Behr, *Way to Nicaea*, 112.

[57] Litfin, "Learning," under "2278."

[58] Ibid.

form can be traced back to this Old Roman Symbol of the second century, giving chronological priority over the Nicene Creed.[59]

Function of the Apostles' Creed

In light of the historical development of the Apostles' Creed, baptismal preparation emerges as the primary function of the creed in its earliest form. Hippolytus presented it in this way as a series of interrogatory questions that were meant to be responded to with the positive affirmation, *I believe*. In the eighth century, Priminius also presented it as an interrogatory baptismal creed. Its usage in baptismal preparation also underscores the catechetical function of the creed. In preparing the candidate for baptism, the creed was used to train new converts of the church. Kelly strongly asserts, "It was precisely this need for formal affirmation of belief to be rehearsed by the catechumen at baptism which instigated the Church to invent creeds in the first place. Whatever other uses they have been put to in the course of history, the true and original use of creeds...was to serve as solemn affirmations of faith in the context of baptismal initiation."[60] While the language of invention might appear too strong, given the creedal development in Scripture already examined in this chapter, the baptismal function of the early forms of the Old Roman Symbol are clear and primary.

The baptismal and catechetical function of the creed highlights what is perhaps the central function of the creedal process in general, which is a summation of the essential elements of the Christian faith. The early church fathers found it necessary to equip new baptismal candidates with the central teachings of the church and not with peripheral matters. Johnson notes that the Apostles' Creed does not present a new theology but rather tells the story of the Christian faith highlighting the main characters and their actions.[61]

The content of the Apostles' Creed shows that this formula also served as a tool against heresy. Although this is not a primary function, Kelly affirms Lebreton's theory that one function of the second-century version of the Old Roman Symbol was to combat Docetism and Adoptionist Monarchianism.[62] While the details of Lebreton's theory are not pertinent here, the function of the Apostles' Creed as a polemic is worthy of note.

This plurality of purposes of the Apostles' Creed serves to highlight the variety of functions a creed can have. While the primary function of the earliest forms of the Old Roman Symbol is baptismal in nature, this has been

---

[59] Gibson, *Three Creeds*, 32. Gibson noted chronological priority of the Apostles' Creed over the Nicene Creed based on the simplicity of the Apostles' Creed and the steps for further explanation taken by the Nicene formulation.

[60] Kelly, *Early Christian Creeds*, 31.

[61] Johnson, *Creed*, 58.

[62] Kelly, *Early Christian Creeds*, 129–30.

shown to not be the only option. As one considers its use in the baptismal ceremony, though, one notes that the use of the interrogatory creed was more than simple liturgy.

The questions accompanied by the positive affirmations of the candidates displayed that they knew and believed, at the very least, these essential identity markers of the Christian faith. This baptismal preparation was training in the essentials, not the peripheral issues of theology. This catechetical function also helps us understand that the creed was not meant to be the sum of theology or the only affirmation of the catechumen. It was rather a foundation and a guide in the much larger theological conversation.

The Nicene Creed

Historical Development

Comparatively, tracing the historical development of the Nicene Creed is a bit clearer and provides defined time periods and key figures involved in the process. It is clear from the outset that the original function of the creed is also very different. While the Apostles' Creed has clear baptismal and catechetical roots, the Nicene Creed formed to address theological concerns.

In reference to the development and function of the Nicene Creed, Turner suggests "The old creeds were creeds for catechumens, the new creed was a creed for bishops."[63] The core theological questions that guided the Council of Nicaea had been swirling around the early church since the time of the apostles and generally revolved around the person and nature of Jesus Christ himself. Who was Jesus in relation to God? How should the phrase *Son of God* be understood? Fuhrmann notes that the early creeds and symbols were clearly Trinitarian, but the exact relationship between the Father, Son, and the Holy Spirit was not clearly defined.[64] Christian theologians in the second and third centuries offered a variety of explanations. As this section traces the historical development of the Nicene Creed, it will first provide a brief sketch of the pre-Nicene theological landscape.

The pre-Nicene theological landscape of the second century displays a surge in the number of voices coming together to answer these large, swirling questions about the exact nature of Jesus in relation to Father. John Meyendorff notes that the second-century church was faced with a "profusion of doctrinal and mystical claims," most coming from Gnostic

---

[63] C. H. Turner, *The History and Use of Creeds and Anathemas in the Early Centuries of the Church*, 2nd ed. (London: Society for Promoting Christian Knowledge, 1910), 24.

[64] Fuhrmann, *Great Creeds of the Church*, 34.

sentiments.[65] Fuhrmann asserts that many of the second-century attempts to answer these questions were rightly guided by a desire to protect the strong monotheism that they saw in the narrative of Scripture.[66]

Often their answers failed though, according to Fuhrmann, because they failed to express the equality with God that Jesus possesses in Scripture as well. Fuhrmann labels those who attempted to protect the oneness of God at all costs as Monarchists and lists Adoptionism or Sabellianism as versions of this view. In this view, God the Father alone is regarded as God and therefore the human Jesus was either "adopted" as the Son of God or was simply a vessel for God to inhabit for a brief time. The Son has no distinction within the Godhead.

Fuhrmann notes that other second-century writers rejected these two views but still failed to fully grasp the nature of equality and distinction. Most notably, Origen taught that Jesus was "God along with and beside God the Father" but he insisted on the distinct subsistence of the Son.[67] John Behr notes that Origen can be a double-sided figure in regard to this topic. In some ways he foreshadows themes later picked up by Arius as in his stress on the distinct subsistence of three divine hypostases, his rejection of the term *homoousios*, and his avoidance of imagery describing the Son as emanating from the Father or being begotten.[68] Yet, he also insisted on the eternal existence of the Son and that God has always been Father, which, according to Behr, paved the way for several key points at Nicaea.[69]

Origen's belief would be carried on by some of his pupils in Alexandria but also challenged by Western leaders like Dionysius of Rome. Fuhrmann, notes that the church in the West had in many ways settled on the consubstantiality of the Trinity, which Tertullian developed in the latter part of the second century.[70] Tertullian taught that the Son and the Spirit were of the same substance, or *homoousios*, as the Father. Those in Alexandria, following Origen's lead, were at first uncomfortable using this type of phrasing, but eventually adopted it to differentiate Jesus from other created beings.

While the church in the West had seemingly accepted the equality of the Son and the Father, there were still those who sought to save a strong

---

[65] John Meyendorff, "The Nicene Creed: Uniting or Dividing Confession," in *Faith to Creed: Ecumenical Perspectives on the Affirmation of the Apostolic Faith in the Fourth Century: Papers of the Faith to Creed Consultation, Commission on Faith and Order, NCCCUSA, October 25–27, 1989–Waltham, Massachusetts*, ed. by S. Mark Heim (Grand Rapids, MI: W.B. Eerdmans for Commission on Faith and Order, National Council of the Churches of Christ in the U.S.A., 1991), 4.

[66] Fuhrmann, *Great Creeds of the Church*, 34–35.

[67] Ibid., 36.

[68] Behr, *Way to Nicaea*, 200.

[69] Ibid., 201.

[70] Fuhrmann, *Great Creeds of the Church*, 36.

monotheistic view of God. The most famous guardian of monotheism at the turn of the fourth century was Arius. Kelly dates what he notes as the "outbreak of the Arian debate" to AD 318, while Arius was a priest at the church of Baucalis.[71] Fuhrmann points out that Arius sought to protect the God of Christianity as "one, ungenerated, and eternal."[72]

Kelly provides us with the strong words of Arius as presented to Bishop Alexander: "We acknowledge one God, Who is alone unbegotten, alone eternal, alone without beginning, alone true, alone possessing immortality, alone wise, alone good, alone ruler, alone judge of all, etc."[73] Arius asserted that the divine essence of God could not be shared with the Son. Therefore, the Son and the Spirit were not of the same substance as the Father. He stressed that they were created beings, emphatically asserting that there was a time when both were not.

Arius's main opponent during this time was the great Athanasius. According to Fuhrmann, Athanasius stressed that if the Son and Spirit were created beings, even if they were created before the beginning of the world, then human beings would have no real contact with God through them.[74] Athanasius also stressed that if the Son were a finite creature he would not be able to comprehend the infinite nature of God. The Son would not truly know the Father and therefore could not fully reveal the Father to humanity. Kelly sums up the Arian point of view contested by Athanasius in this way: "The net result was [that] the Trinity, or divine Trias, was described, in speciously Origenistic language, as consisting of three Persons. But, the three Persons were three utterly different beings, and did not share in any way the same substance or essence as each other."[75]

The Council of Nicaea, which was assembled by Constantine to provide unity for the church in the spring of AD 325, provided a definitive answer and resolution for this debate by developing a formal creed refuting the claims of Arianism. While the exact details of the council are lost to history since no official transcripts of the meetings were ever released, the text of the creed that was produced by this council exists and its very particular wording is telling of the events of the proceedings. The ecumenical nature of the council affirms that the Nicene Creed stands as the first ecumenical creed of the church. Leith notes that the Council of Nicaea marked a new stage in creedal development.[76]

---

[71] Kelly, *Early Christian Creeds*, 231.
[72] Fuhrmann, *Great Creeds of the Church*, 37.
[73] Kelly, *Early Christian Creeds*, 232.
[74] Fuhrmann, *Great Creeds of the Church*, 43. For Athanasius, both the true divinity of Jesus along with his true humanity in the incarnation were imperative for Christ's soteriological work. See *On the Incarnation of the Word*.
[75] Kelly, *Early Christian Creeds*, 234.
[76] Leith, *Creeds of the Church*, 28.

It would be incorrect, though, to assert that the Council of Nicaea created the famous creed out of nothing. It clearly resembles the baptismal creeds that have been shown to be common since at least the early second century. Meyendorff points out that as the church began to formalize its belief at the council, it remained faithful to the baptismal contexts of earlier creeds.[77] Kelly notes that these earlier baptismal creeds were mostly localized expressions and therefore it was important for the church to bring these formulations together into a unified voice.[78] Scholars have suggested that either the baptismal creed of Palestinian Caesarea or the creed of Jerusalem most likely served as the basis for the creed formulated at Nicaea.[79]

Between the Council of Nicaea and the current form of the Nicene Creed lies another important step, the Council of Constantinople in AD 381. The earlier version of the creed was further refined at this council. It will be helpful to compare the texts of each creed to note the significant additions. The text of the Council of Nicaea's creed is as follows:

We believe in one God, the Father Almighty, Maker of all things visible and invisible.

And in one Lord Jesus Christ , the Son of God, begotten of the Father [the only-begotten; that is, of the essence of the Father, God of God], Light of Light, very God of very God, begotten, not made, being of one substance (*homoousion*) with the Father; by whom all things were made [both in heaven and on earth]; who for us men, and for our salvation, came down and was incarnate and was made man; he suffered, and the third day he rose again, ascended into heaven; from thence he shall come to judge the quick and the dead.

And in the Holy Ghost.

[But those who say: 'There was a time when he was not;' and 'He was not before he was made;' and 'He was made out of nothing,' or 'He is of another substance' or 'essence,' or 'The Son of God is created,' or

---

[77] Meyendorff, "The Nicene Creed," 8.

[78] Kelly, *Early Christian Creeds*, 205.

[79] Fuhrmann, *Great Creeds of the Church*, 40. Kelly rejects the notion that the creed of Caesarea served as the basis and others follow his lead. See Kelly, *Early Christian Creeds*, 217–20. A growing majority of scholars now lean toward the creed of Jerusalem. See Meyendorff, 9. Craig Blaising rejects the notion that a baptismal creed serves as the foundation for the Nicene Creed. Blaising, instead, argues that the Creed is a hermeneutical development in understanding the *Shema* and 1 Corinthians 6:8. See Craig A. Blaising, "Creedal Development as Hermeneutical Development: A Reexamination of Nicaea," *Pro Ecclesia* XIX, no. 4 (2010): 381–82.

'changeable,' or 'alterable'—they are condemned by the holy catholic and apostolic Church.]"[80]

The text of the Constantinopolitan Creed is as follows:

We believe in one God, the Father Almighty, Maker of *heaven and earth, and of all* things visible and invisible.

And in one Lord Jesus Christ , the *only-begotten* Son of God, begotten of the Father *before all worlds* (æons), Light of Light, very God of very God, begotten, not made, being of one substance with the Father; by whom all things were made; who for us men, and for our salvation, came down *from heaven*, and was incarnate *by the Holy Ghost of the Virgin Mary*, and was made man; he *was crucified for us under Pontius Pilate*, and suffered, *and was buried*, and the third day he rose again, *according to the Scriptures*, and ascended into heaven, *and sitteth on the right hand of the Father*; from thence he shall come *again, with glory*, to judge the quick and the dead; *whose kingdom shall have no end.*

And in the Holy Ghost, *the Lord and Giver of life, who proceedeth from the Father, who with the Father and the Son together is worshiped and glorified, who spake by the prophets. In one holy catholic and apostolic Church; we acknowledge one baptism for the remissi*on of sins; we look for the resurrection of the dead, and the life of the world to come. Amen.[81]

As one can see, the later Constantinopolitan Creed further develops several key points in the creed. Most notably, this version develops the understanding of the Holy Spirit from one line plus an anathema to several lines that give further detail to essential affirmations concerning the person of the Holy Spirit. The Constantinopolitan version of the creed represents the current form of what is considered the Nicene Creed and was officially affirmed at the Council of Chalcedon in AD 451.[82] At Chalcedon, the Nicene Creed was accepted by both the church in the West and the church in the East, marking its unique status as an ecumenical statement of belief. While the addition of the *et filioque* in AD 589 caused division between the East and the West, it does not negate the ecumenical nature of the early form of the creed.

---

[80] This text is drawn from Schaff, *The Creeds of Christendom*, 28–29. One may notice how abruptly this version of the creed ends with one short sentence on the Holy Spirit, followed by an anathema for those who dispute it.

[81] This text is drawn from Schaff, *The Creeds of Christendom*, 28–29. Italics were used by Schaff to note the differences.

[82] Leith, *Creeds of the Churches*, 31. See also Schaff, *The Creeds of Christendom*, 29–30.

Function of the Nicene Creed

It is clear from the historical origins of the Nicene Creed that its formulation carried with it a particular task or function, that is, to serve as a test for orthodoxy. Kelly observes that the Nicene Creed and others that would follow during the fourth century "were put forth not merely as epitomes of the beliefs of their promulgators, but as test of orthodoxy of Christians in general."[83] This function marked a transition from the localized baptismal creeds that preceded the Nicene period.

The formulation of the Nicene Creed served as a statement to those, like Arius, who taught other views on the nature of Jesus and the Holy Spirit. Fuhrmann notes that the use of the term *substance (ousia)* twice displays a clear rebuke of Arian thought.[84] Gibson notes that the particular language used displays the need felt by those present at Nicaea to further development the theological language used to talk about God.[85] The simple baptismal formulas of the past simply would not work against the likes of Arius. Further clarification as to the precise relationship of the Father to the Son was needed to fully grasp the biblical conception of God.

Another function of the Nicene Creed, as evidenced by the formation of the Council in Nicaea, was ecumenical unity. The creed was designed to bring the church universal together in agreement concerning the key essentials of Christian belief. Leith notes, though, that this unity did not occur at once, but rather over a fifty-year period after the council while the creed was debated and examined further.[86] With the affirmation of the creed by the Council of Constantinople, a more widespread ecumenical unity was achieved.

The wide acceptance of the creed and its continual usage of the creed by both the church in the West and the church in the East underscores its unifying power. The ecumenical unity noted here is not meant to disregard further debates or controversies. Young asserts that the political and imperial nature of the first council in Nicaea only exacerbated division but this statement seems unsupported, given the broad acceptance of the creed within a relatively short period of time.[87] In any light, the Nicene

---

[83] Kelly, *Early Christian Creeds*, 205. Young asserts that it is important to note that the pre-Nicene creeds did not originate as tests of orthodoxy but rather as simple summaries of the three main characters of Christian story. The later political, philosophical, and theological pressures that surrounded the Council of Nicaea led to this shift in function. See Young, *Making of the Creeds*, 11–13.

[84] Fuhrmann, *Great Creeds of the Church*, 41.

[85] Gibson, *Three Creeds*, 32.

[86] Leith, *Creeds of the Churches*, 29.

[87] Young, *Making of the Creeds*, 13.

Creed stands tall as a great achievement of the church universal and a lasting summation of the essential identity markers of the Christian faith.

Conclusion

In this brief survey of the historical development of the creedal process and the various functions of the creeds themselves several key points emerge. First, the later, formal creeds of the Christian church have roots in the creedal material found in Scripture. They cannot be mere inventions of the second- through fourth-century church. Second, the creedal statements in Scripture and the later creeds served to clearly identify the God whom Christians worship and serve. This identification of God also distinguished Christianity from other religions. Finally, the overarching primary function of the creedal process was to identify and articulate the core identity markers of the Christian message. This process of identification and articulation will be mirrored in the EIM model constructed in this book.

2

Case Study 1 —
Trinity and Christology in the Creeds

As noted in the previous chapters, the development of the great creeds of the Christian faith reflects the arduous process of identifying and articulating the central identity markers of Christianity drawn from the Scriptures and carried on through the tradition of the church. The central identity markers articulated by the early church provide the foundation for the great doctrines of the church, none more central than the doctrine of the Trinity. Trinitarian theology is vitally important for the greater theological conversation because it identities just exactly who the God of the Christian faith is. One must keep in mind, though, that Trinitarian thought spawned from the initial question of who Jesus is.

The establishment of a strong Christology inevitably leads to a greater understanding of God as Triune. From its origin, Christianity has been intricately tied to the person and work of Jesus Christ. C. S. Lewis states that Christianity is not the result of a long, drawn-out philosophical debate but rather a catastrophic historical event (the life, death, and resurrection of Jesus Christ).[1] Since Christianity cannot be separated from Christ, Trinitarian thought and Christology must go hand in hand and must be properly understood to fully grasp the God of the Christian faith. Error in either of these doctrines will drastically affect every other aspect of the theological conversation.

The creedal development of the early church exposes the importance of both Trinitarian theology and Christology. The development of both Trinitarian theology and Christology leading up to the creeds is also an extremely valuable window into the process of theological discourse. Franz Dünzl reminds us that the Christian confession of a triune God was not invented by the later fourth century creeds nor was it explicitly given by the apostles to be protected and preserved by the church. "Rather, this confession grew out of the living tradition of the church in a three-hundred-year-long history, in which generations of theologians and believers took

---

[1] C. S. Lewis, *The Problem of Pain* (New York: HarperOne, 2001), 15.

part."[2] This long conversation included all voices and all attempts to understand God as one as well as Father, Son, and Spirit. Many of the paths proved to be dead ends, yet they are vital parts of the process. Many of the dead ends, which have now been condemned by the church, gave greater clarity to the right way of articulating these deep truths about the nature of God as revealed in the biblical narrative.

While firmly grounded in Scripture these two great theological doctrines were molded and shaped during the apostolic and patristic periods leading up to the formation of the early creeds. The process of identifying and articulating the essential identity markers of each doctrine was a dialogue between assenting and dissenting voices with the ultimate guide being the biblical narrative. Kelly notes that this period stands as a formative age for theology, which "exhibited the extremes of immaturity and sophistication."[3] A closer examination of this dialogue will serve as an important case study.

This chapter will trace the theological development of Trinitarian and Christological thought from creedal formulations found in the biblical text through the later apostolic and patristic periods leading up to the Council of Constantinople in AD 381, before summarizing the primary affirmations of Scripture that shaped these periods. Following this summary, a survey of various theological voices that further developed the understanding of the doctrine of the Trinity will be presented before concluding with several implications for teaching these specific doctrines today using the EIM model. The purpose for this case study is to better understand the creedal process and therefore better understand how to apply this creedal process to each subcategory of systematic theology.

Historical Development (Apostolic Period to Constantinople)

Monotheistic Roots of Christianity

In his work *Faith Seeking Understanding*, Daniel Migliore asserts that the doctrine of the Trinity is not a revealed doctrine of the church; rather it is the result of theological inquiry and discovery.[4] It is a doctrine that was developed and shaped by the theological discourse of the apostolic and

---

[2] Franz Dünzl, *A Brief History of the Doctrine of the Trinity in the Early Church* (London: T & T Clark, 2007), x.

[3] J. N. D. Kelly, *Early Christian Doctrines* (New York: Harper, 1959), 3.

[4] Daniel L. Migliore, *Faith Seeking Understanding: An Introduction to Christian Theology* (Grand Rapids, MI: W.B. Eerdmans, 1991), 69. Migliore goes on to elaborate on his meaning. "It did not descend miraculously from heaven, nor was it written by God on tablets of stone. It is the product of the meditation and reflection of the church on the gospel message over many centuries."

patristic periods. The "unrevealed" status of the doctrine should not detract from its veracity. Dünzl observes that it seems logical that God would not want to communicate himself beyond human comprehension but rather that he would "use the (limited) power of our thoughts and feelings, our (incomplete) striving for knowledge, our creativity and even our delight in disputation to disclose himself in the garb of human thoughts and words."[5] It is a doctrine that theologians have had to work out, and in doing, so they have been drawn deeper into the story of God.

The development of Trinitarian and Christological thought over the first three hundred years of the church provides a surprising conclusion given the monotheistic foundation upon which it was built. Christianity was and is and always has been a monotheistic religion. This is affirmed in the Shema of the Hebrew Bible: "Hear, O Israel: The Lord is our God, the Lord alone. You shall love the Lord your God with all your heart, and with all your soul, and with all your might" (Deut 6:4–5). It is also reaffirmed in the pages of the New Testament.

In the Gospels, Jesus emphasizes the Shema in understanding the greatest commandment (Mark 12:29–34). Paul continually stresses the oneness of God (i.e., Rom 3:30, 1 Cor 8:4–6, Gal 3:20, Eph 4:6). James also stresses God as one: "You believe that God is one; you do well. Even the demons believe—and shudder" (James 2:19). This monotheistic foundation, though, instead of leading one away from Trinitarian thought serves as an essential identity marker that guided and shaped, and eventually forced, this surprising and wonderful conclusion.

In developing his cultural-linguistic approach to the nature of doctrine, George Lindbeck notes at least three "regulative principles" at play in the development of the Trinitarian nature of the early creeds: the monotheistic principle, the principle of historical specificity, and the principle of Christological maximalism.[6] For Lindbeck the principle of monotheism stands as the initial guiding principle. For early Christians, "there was only one God, the God of Abraham, Isaac, Jacob, and Jesus."[7] This monotheistic principle, along with the other regulative principles, guided the theological conversation and served as a criterion for discovering the articulation of the doctrine of the Trinity that most closely reflected the biblical narrative. Lindbeck concludes,

It can thus be argued that the Nicene and Chalcedonian formulations were among the few, and perhaps the only, possible outcomes of the process of adjusting Christian discourse to the world of late classical antiquity in a manner comfortable to regulative principles that were

---

[5] Dünzl, *Brief History*, x–xi.

[6] Lindbeck, *Nature of Doctrine*, 80–81.

[7] Ibid., 80.

already at work in the earliest strata of the tradition. These creeds can be understood by Christian and non-Christian alike as paradigmatically instantiating doctrinal rules that have been abidingly important from the beginning in forming mainstream Christian identity.[8]

Lindbeck's conclusion underscores the effect of regulative principles on theological discourse. In this book, regulative principles will be replaced by essential identity markers, but in many ways will serve the same function in guiding theological discourse in a foreseeable direction.

The monotheistic foundation of the Christian faith does conjure certain questions. How did the earliest Christians begin to nuance their understanding of the oneness of God? How did a strict monotheistic religion, as highlighted in Isa 44:6—"I am the first and I am the last; besides me there is no god"—give birth to a triune understanding of this one God? Oscar Cullmann notes that among the confessions of primitive Christianity, the slogan "Jesus is Lord" (*Kurios Iēsous*) is the earliest.[9] While some have criticized Cullmann for disregarding the priority of the Shema, his recognition of the Christological focus of primitive Christianity holds.[10] With the emergence of this slogan Christian theologians began to wrestle with the exact relationship between the Father and the Son. Many of the earliest Christian articulations of God are predominately binitarian in nature (Father and Son) in response to this slogan. If Jesus is Lord, then how does that change one's understanding of who God is?

Dünzl also affirms that Trinitarian thought begins with affirmations about the person and work of Christ.[11] Citing Paul's use of an earlier creedal formula in Rom 1:3–4, Dünzl notes that after the resurrection the Christian community began to deepen their understanding of the nature of Jesus Christ. In this passage, Paul affirms the earlier tradition that Jesus was not only the Messiah from the line of David but also the Son of God in power as signified by the resurrection. Dünzl stresses that this recognition of Jesus as Son of God became descriptive of Jesus overall not just after the resurrection, noting the various Gospel references to Jesus as Son of God (Mark 1:9–11; 9:7; 15:39; Matt 1:20; Luke 1:35). This Christological focus had great implications for the theological discourse of the nature of God.

To understand how followers of a strict monotheistic religion like Judaism could also begin to include Jesus in their conception of God, Richard Bauckham has proposed a divine-identity Christology. Bauckham proposes that the formation of a high Christology was possible within a

---

[8] Lindbeck, *Nature of Doctrine*, 81.

[9] Cullmann, *Earliest Christian Confessions*, 57.

[10] See Malcolm B. Yarnell, *The Formation of Christian Doctrine* (Nashville, TN: B & H Academic, 2007), 145. See also Pelikan, *Credo*, 130.

[11] Dünzl, *Brief History*, 3–4.

Jewish monotheistic context not because the earliest Christians applied some divine status to Jesus but rather, they identified him directly with the one God of Israel.[12]

Bauckham stresses that identification with the unique God of Israel was the central concern, rather than understanding divine nature. "In other words, for Jewish monotheistic belief what was important was *who* the one God is, rather than what divinity is" (emphasis in original).[13] Bauckham notes that by identifying Jesus with actions that alone were the God of Israel's, like creation, forgiveness of sins, and eschatological redemption, the earliest Christians were proposing a high Christology. Bauckham cites five texts where Paul cites the Hebrew Bible and identifies Jesus with YHWH (Rom 10:13 [Joel 2:32]; 1 Cor 1:31 [Jer 9:24]; 1 Cor 2:16 [Isa 40:13]; 1 Cor 10:26 [Ps 23]; 2 Cor 10:17 [Jer 9:24]).[14]

This identification of Jesus with the YHWH of Israel, as seen in the writings of Paul and John, was not accepted by all early Christian sects, however. Dünzl notes that various sects like the Ebionites, instead of harmonizing the message of the Gospels with Paul, chose to focus on one aspect of the Gospel of Mark and therefore asserted that Jesus was just a man who was adopted as the Son of God at the baptism.[15] Beyond the Ebionites, Dünzl highlights Theodotus of Byzantium, Theodotus the Younger, and Artemon as proponents of an adoptionistic Christology.

In the context of a strict monotheism, adoptionism does hold certain advantages but was ultimately rejected by the church because it fails to explain the complexity of the entire Gospel narrative of Jesus, especially his identification with the unique God of Israel time and time again. Dünzl highlights another dissenting voice in the theological discourse of this early period as that of the Gnostics, who viewed the spiritual element of Jesus as divine but disassociated him from the Jewish creator God.[16] For the

---

[12] Richard Bauckham, "Paul's Christology of Divine Identity" (paper presented at the annual meeting of the Society of Biblical Literature, Toronto, Canada, November 25, 2002, 2. Available online at http://www.forananswer.org/Top_JW/Ricahrd_Bauckham.pdf.

[13] Ibid.

[14] Ibid., 5.

[15] Dünzl, *Brief History*, 8. See also Jaroslav Pelikan, *The Christian Tradition: A History of the Development of Doctrine: The Emergence of the Catholic Tradition, 100–600*, vol. 1 (Chicago, IL: University of Chicago Press, 1971), 176.

[16] Dünzl, *Brief History*, 9. In using the term *Gnostic*, Dünzl is identifying the second-century belief system that separates true divinity from the created/material world, therefore affecting the nature of the Incarnation. Dünzl does note that Gnostic thought was highly divergent in particular details but carried this one overarching theme. We will follow Dünzl understanding in this section. It should be noted here that current scholarship is divided on the exact usage of the terms *Gnostics* and *Gnosticism*. For a deeper discussion, See Carl B. Smith, "Post-Bauer Scholarship on Gnosticism(s): The Current State of Our 'Knowledge,'" in *Orthodoxy and Heresy in Early Christian*

Gnostics, Jesus represented a connection to a transcendent God who was far removed from the material world. Again, this view failed to account for the entire scope of the biblical narrative on Jesus and God's relation to the material world.

In noting these two dissenting voices in terms of their incongruence with the entirety of the biblical message, it would also be good to note the source of the biblical message during this early apostolic era. Questions arise regarding the exact nature of the biblical message during this time, for the writings of the New Testament had just been completed and the canon of Scripture had not been fully recognized. What were the sources used by the apostolic fathers to understand the right belief system and to refute these dissenting voices? Kelly notes that when one surveys the writings of Clement of Rome, Ignatius, or Polycarp, an appeal to both the Hebrew Bible and the apostles' writings characterized the age, citing Polycarp's letter to the Philippians, where he urged them to accept "the apostles who preached the gospel to us and the prophets who announced our Lord's coming in advance."[17]

He goes on to stress that "the importance of the Old Testament as a doctrinal norm in the primitive Church cannot be exaggerated."[18] The Hebrew Bible, especially read in light of the Jesus story, served as a foundation of doctrine. This becomes extremely evident in the rejection of Marcion and his followers in the middle of the second century. The apostles' writings are held in the same light and noted by Polycarp and Justin. Kelly notes that this emphasis on the apostles' teachings must not be confined to just the written documents, asserting mostly as an argument from silence that the oral tradition would have influenced the shape of the doctrine as well.[19]

In terms of the development of Trinitarian and Christological thought, Kelly notes that the earliest of the apostolic fathers offer but mere seeds of later more developed thought, noting recognition of God, Christ, and Spirit in various triadic formulas but no further explanation as to the exact relation between the three. For Kelly, the major contribution of these early fathers is the affirmation of the preexistence of Christ and his work with the Father in the act of creation.[20] This sets up Christ as equal with God

---

Contexts: Reconsidering the Bauer Thesis, edited by Paul Hartog (Eugene, Scotland: Pickwick, 2015).

[17] Kelly, *Early Christian Doctrines*, 31. See also Polycarp, *Phil. 6.3.*

[18] Kelly, *Early Christian Doctrines*, 32.

[19] Ibid., 33. Here Kelly's argument from silence seems weak but it is logical to assume the priority of the oral tradition over the written and therefore somewhat safe to assume that at this time the oral tradition was still an influencing power on theological discourse.

[20] Kelly, *Early Christian Doctrines*, 92.

and opens the door for further conversation about the nature of this relationship.

Justin Martyr (c. AD 112–165)

As one traces the line from Christology to Trinity, Justin Martyr emerges as a key figure of the second century. Justin concerned himself with defending the Christian faith in a way that stood up to philosophical scrutiny. Therefore, he is known as one of the Apologists. Behr asserts that with the writings of Justin one enters "a very different world" than with writings of the apostles and apostolic fathers like Ignatius and Polycarp, observing that the latter wrote mainly to Christian communities while Justin began to dialogue with the greater world.[21]

Amidst the apologetic argumentation of Justin's writings, one also begins to see an unfolding understanding of Scripture and theology. Behr notes that Justin is more explicit than writers like Ignatius in attempting to relate the kerygma, the passed-down tradition of the apostles, with Scripture.[22]

In Justin's developing theology one sees stronger statements on the nature of Jesus and his connection with Hebrew Bible prophecy, as well as a coming together of Father and Jesus as Son of God. In his *Apology*, Justin asserted, "We say that the Word, who is the first offspring of God, was begotten without carnal intercourse, Jesus Christ our teacher, and that He was crucified, and died, and rose again, and ascended to heaven."[23] Here one can note the creedal nature of his statement.

In his *Dialogue with Trypho*, he made a stronger case, stating, "The Father of the universe has a Son: who also, being the first begotten Word of God, is even God. And of old He appeared in the shape of fire and in the likeness of an angel to Moses and to the other prophets; but now in the times of your reign, having, as we before said, become Man by a virgin."[24] In *Dialogue* Justin defended the gospel of Jesus in a Jewish context and attempted to bring together the concept of Jewish monotheism, which was shared by the Christians, and Jesus as the Son of God.

Behr notes that in the writings of Justin one notices a deep search to explain how Jesus and God the Father and Maker of all are both God and yet distinct from each other.[25] In *Dialogue*, Justin asserted to Trypho,

---

[21] Behr, *Way to Nicaea*, 93.

[22] Ibid., 94–96. It is worth noting here that by Scripture, Justin was primarily working with the writings of the Hebrew Bible. He does also engage with the writings of the apostles, especially the Synoptic Gospels.

[23] Justin Martyr, *Apology* 21.1.

[24] Justin Martyr, *Dialogue with Trypho* 36.

[25] Behr, *Nicaea*, 104.

I shall endeavour to persuade you that he who is said to have appeared to Abraham and to Jacob and to Moses, is an additional God to him who made all things—distinct numerically, I mean, not distinct in will. For I affirm that he has never at any time done or said anything which he who made the world—above whom there is no other God—has not wished him both to do and to engage himself with.[26]

In many ways he appears to be describing a form of subordinationism where Jesus is God but lower than the Father who could not present himself on earth. This subordinationist tendency of Justin was clarified by later writers. Dünzl notes that this assertion of two Gods offends the strict notion of monotheism of the time, and to resolve the offense, Justin appealed to the Logos Christology in John's Gospel as well as Greek philosophy.[27] Writing to a pagan audience, Justin believed the concept of the Logos would be a sufficient way to explain Jesus Christ.

For Justin, the Logos, or the Word of God, was the preexistent, second person of the Holy Triad and was the way God revealed Godself to the world. James Papandrea notes that for Justin, "the Son is the Father's *Angel*, not in the sense of a created being, but in the sense of the literal meaning of the Greek word *angelos*, meaning 'messenger' or 'agent,' and so the hierarchy is one of Sender and Messenger."[28] While Justin stressed the unity in divinity of the Father and the Son, his focus on the distinction later struck some as a subordination.

The subordinationist tendency in Justin's writings highlights the complex nature of the development of Trinitarian thought. A step away from one heretical leaning could move the theologian closer to another form. A move to stress the distinction of the three persons could be perceived as move against unity. A move to preserve the unity of God could move the theologian into a modalistic vision of the Godhead, much like the teachings of Noetus or Sabellius.[29] The theological discourse of this time will be marked by this back-and-forth movement, with each step offering greater clarity.

Irenaeus of Lyons (c. AD 125–202)

The next voice to emerge in the great theological conversation of the second century was Irenaeus of Lyons. Though he was a bishop in the West,

---

[26] *Dialogue*, 56.11.

[27] Dünzl, *Brief History*, 22.

[28] James L. Papandrea, *The Earliest Christologies: Five Images of Christ in the Postapostolic Age* (Downers Grove, IL: IVP Academic, 2016), 93. See also Justin Martyr, *1 Apology* 63.

[29] Dünzl, *Brief History*, 28.

Irenaeus grew up in the East and learned from early apostolic fathers such as Polycarp, whom Irenaeus himself noted received the gospel from Jesus's very eyewitnesses, the Apostles, who retold the story of Jesus in agreement with the Scriptures.[30] Behr observes that Irenaeus used this foundation, "the Gospel 'according to the Scriptures' as delivered in the beginning by the apostles," to seek unity among the various forms of primitive Christianity.[31]

According to Behr, this commitment to a common body of Scripture, which included the writings of the apostles stands as "the most significant transition in early Christianity."[32] Irenaeus used this foundation to gauge other teachings and theologies swirling around during the second century. Did they match up with both the writings of the Hebrew Bible and with the tradition of the apostles?

For Irenaeus, the subordinationist leanings of Justin Martyr and others did not match up with the biblical narrative. Though he does not specifically criticize Justin or other apostolic fathers, Irenaeus strongly rejected any form of subordination within the Holy Triad. For him, the claim of Jesus, "Anyone who has seen me has seen the Father" (John 14:9), would be false if he were in anyway subordinate to the Father. Behr notes that for Irenaeus, "such subordination would destroy the whole economy: if God himself has not become visible in his Son, Jesus Christ, then no real communion between God and man has been established."[33] This connection between Father and Son in revelation was picked up and staunchly defended by Athanasius and used as a main argument against Arians.[34]

Irenaeus does build on the foundation laid by Justin in terms of the revelation of God in the Hebrew Bible. For Justin, it was the task of Jesus to reveal the Father because the Father could not become visible on earth. Irenaeus stressed that Son and Father are united in this revelation. He stressed, "Christ Himself therefore, together with the Father, is the God of the living, who spoke to Moses, and who was also manifested to the fathers."[35] In bringing the Father and Son together in this act of revelation, Irenaeus added another layer to the complex foundation of emerging Trinitarian thought. Bernhard Lohse notes that in Irenaeus one sees the most fully developed doctrine of the Trinity of the first and second centuries.[36]

---

[30] *Against Heresies* 3.3.4.

[31] Behr, *Nicaea*, 111.

[32] Ibid.

[33] Ibid., 104.

[34] See Roger E. Olson, *The Story of Christian Theology: Twenty Centuries of Tradition & Reform* (Downers Grove, IL: InterVarsity Press, 1999), 161–72. Here, Olsen also notes the soteriological reasons for Athanasius's emphasis on the unity of the Father and Son.

[35] Irenaeus, *Against Heresies* 4.5.2.

[36] Bernhard Lohse, *A Short History of Christian Doctrine* (Philadelphia, PA: Fortress Press, 1966), 44.

Irenaeus's developed theology can be seen in his recognition of a Rule of Faith passed down from the apostles. In *Against Heresies*, he reconstructs this Rule of Faith as:

> believing in one God, the Creator of heaven and earth, and all things therein, by means of Christ Jesus, the Son of God; who, because of His surpassing love towards His creation, condescended to be born of the virgin, He Himself uniting man through Himself to God, and having suffered under Pontius Pilate, and rising again, and having been received up in splendour, shall come in glory, the Saviour of those who are saved, and the Judge of those who are judged, and sending into eternal fire those who transform the truth, and despise His Father and His advent.[37]

In this Rule, Irenaeus clearly affirmed the identity marker of one God and held Christ as the Son of God, through whom everything was created. In the context preceding this quotation, he also noted the work of the Spirit in writing this rule on the hearts of men who do not have the written word of God. Mary Ann Donovan observes how this Rule underlies the very structure of Irenaeus's writing *Against Heresies* as well as his overall theology.[38]

Tertullian of Carthage (c. AD 145–225)

Further development of the doctrine of the Trinity is seen in the writings of the Latin father, Tertullian. With Tertullian an explicit Trinitarian framework begins to takes shape, one that will have a lasting effect on the language of the conversation. George Léonard Prestige notes that Tertullian, unlike the Greek Fathers who tended to be nuanced in their explanations, plainly refers to the various persons of the Godhead as *God* and is the first to use the term *trinitas* in the West.[39] Lohse notes that Tertullian is first to provide the formula of the unity of the Godhead plus distinction of persons.[40]

With the term *trinitas*, Tertullian stressed the distinction of each person of the Godhead against any form of Sabellian modalistic thought,

---

[37] Irenaeus, *Against Heresies* 3.4.2 (See also 1.10.1). English translation from Philip Schaff, *Ante Nicene Fathers Volume 1.*

[38] Mary Ann Donovan, *One Right Reading? A Guide to Irenaeus* (Collegeville, MN: Liturgical Press, 1997), 11–17.

[39] G. L. Prestige, *God in Patristic Thought*, trans. F. L. Cross (London: S.P.C.K., 1952), 93. Here, Prestige gives a concise survey of the usage of terms like *triad* and *trinitas* in the second century.

[40] Lohse, *A Short History*, 45.

especially in his treatise *Against Praxeas*. In response to this modalistic thought, Tertullian noted, "All are of One, by unity (that is) of substance; while the mystery of the dispensation is still guarded, which distributes the Unity into a Trinity, placing in their order the three *Persons*— the Father, the Son, and the Holy Ghost."[41] He brought greater clarity to the concept of distinction by noting that the three persons are distinct, "not in condition, but in degree; not in substance, but in form; not in power, but in aspect."[42]

For Tertullian, this unity and distinction form the essential identity markers of the biblical narrative of God, a narrative that stresses the oneness of God as well as the economy of Father, Son, and Spirit. For Prestige, Tertullian rests his doctrine on the concept of economy, "that unity constitutes the triad out of its own inherent nature, not by any process of sub-division, but by reason of a principle of constructive integration which the godhead essentially possesses."[43] Prestige asserts that for Tertullian his concept of unity is not mathematical but rather philosophical.[44]

Kelly notes that Tertullian expresses this unity in terms of substance, terminology that, as has been noted, will influence further Trinitarian development.[45] It is interesting to note that Tertullian was largely binarian in his thinking and writing. Andrew McGowan keenly notes that perhaps it is Tertullian's allegiance to the New Prophecy, later known as Montanism, with its particular focus on the Holy Spirit, that rounds out his more complete Trinitarian thought.[46]

Tertullian's use of the Rule of Faith also provides a clear picture of the development of the doctrines of the Trinity and Christology up to the middle of the third century. In his treatise *Prescriptions Against Heretics*, he clearly laid out his rendition of the Rule:

There is but one God, who is none other than the Creator of the world, who produced everything from nothing through his Word, sent forth before all things; that this Word is called his Son, and in the Name of God was seen in divers ways by the patriarchs, was ever heard in the prophets and finally was brought down by the Spirit and Power of God the Father into the Virgin Mary, was made flesh in her womb, was born of her and lived as Jesus Christ; who thereafter proclaimed a new law and a new promise of the kingdom of heaven, worked miracles, was

---

[41] Tertullian, *Against Praxeas* Chapter 2.

[42] Ibid.

[43] Prestige, *God in Patristic Thought*, 99.

[44] Ibid.

[45] Kelly, *Early Christian Doctrine*, 115.

[46] Andrew Brian McGowan, "Tertullian and the 'Heretical' Origins of the 'Orthodox' Trinity," *Journal of Early Christian Studies* 14, no. 4 (2006): 437–57.

crucified, on the third day rose again, was caught up into heaven and sat down at the right hand of the Father; that he sent in his place the power of the Holy Spirit to guide believers; that he will come with glory to take the saints up into the fruition of the life eternal and the heavenly promises and to judge the wicked to everlasting fire, after the resurrection of both good and evil with the restoration of their flesh.[47]

In Tertullian's version of the Rule one sees clear essential identity markers of Christian theology that guided his own theological inquiry. Bryan Litfin notes that not only did the Rule of Faith guide Tertullian's theology it also served as the key aspect of his apologetic argument against heretical teaching.[48] Tertullian used the Rule to measure and assess and refute the heretical teachings of his day, for it captured the essential identity markers of the Christian faith.

Origen of Alexandria (c. AD 184–253)

After Tertullian, Origen of Alexandria emerges early in the third century as a powerful and influential voice in the development of Trinitarian thought. Unlike Irenaeus and Tertullian, Origen enjoys a complicated history in the long and unfolding theological discourse of the church. In some ways, his contributions still influence the conversation. Roger Olsen asserts that some of the greatest heroes of orthodoxy, like Athanasius, were influenced by Origen.[49]

Yet in other ways Origen set up a misunderstanding of the nature of the Trinity that was later carried on by the Arians and other heretical teachings. Lohse notes that, much like Irenaeus and Tertullian, Origen stresses the unity of God, but he also, and this is where he lends to error, stresses the distinction of the three in such a way that the Son and the Spirit are more subordinate to the Father instead of equal.[50] Origen utilized the concept of *homoousios* to express the oneness of being in the Godhead and *hypostasis* to express the three persons, but in his understanding of hypostasis Origen leaves the door open to further separation of the Godhead.

Origen, like Irenaeus and Tertullian, also gave us a complete rendition of the Rule of Faith and allowed the Rule to guide and shape his theology. In his preface to his treatise *On First Principles*, Origen provided

---

[47] Tertullian, *Prescriptions Against Heretics* 13; trans. Greenslade, *Early Latin Theology*, 40.

[48] Litfin, "Learning," under "2281."

[49] Olsen, *Story of Christian Theology*, 100.

[50] Lohse, *A Short History*, 46. Olsen notes that the Holy Spirit was neglect if not ignored in most of Origen's writings on the Trinity, perhaps another example of his tendency to subordination. See Olsen, *Story of Christian Theology*, 108.

two sets of information in which he distinguishes what is essential and has been passed on from the apostolic tradition and what is open for debate.[51] In the first category, Origen clearly listed Father, Son, and Holy Spirit as distinct yet unified in deity. But with the latter section, Origen provided the space necessary for further theological investigation. He particularly noted that it is unclear if the Holy Spirit should also be considered a Son of God and that more inquiry into the Scriptures is needed.[52] Litfin notes that Origen used the Rule to affirm the essential elements of apostolic teaching carried on in church tradition, but also to leave room for further debate and inquiry.[53]

The Arian Controversy

The immediate context of the Council of Nicaea and the formation of the great Nicene Creed is the Arian controversy involving the "arch-heretic" Arius, a presbyter over the district of Baucalis in Alexandria, and Alexander the bishop of Alexandria, along with the staunch preserver of orthodoxy Athanasius, Alexander's assistant.[54] Dünzl notes that the controversy broke out around 318 as a dispute between Arius and Alexander and involved the interpretation of a particular Hebrew Bible passage, Proverbs 8:22–25.[55] In Proverbs 8:22–25 Wisdom attributes her own creation to God as God then uses Wisdom to create the rest of the world. For Arius this unlocked the answer of where Jesus, as the Logos of God, fit into the doctrine of God.

Arius proposed that Jesus was created by God, the first of God's creations but created nonetheless, therefore dividing the unity of God as stressed by Irenaeus and Tertullian. In contrast to eternal generation from the Father, Arius asserted that there was a time when the Son was not. Kelly notes that the fundamental premise of Arius's theology was the "absolute uniqueness and transcendence of God, the unoriginated source of all reality."[56] Arius believed that for God to impart God's own substance to another being would mean that God is divisible and therefore not God. Since

---

[51] Origen, *On First Principles* 1.pref.4–10; trans. *ANF04*.

[52] Ibid., 1.pref.4.

[53] Litfin, "Learning," under "2396." Litfin also notes that Origen includes elements in his rendition of the Rule that were not seen in earlier renditions, such as the free will of the soul, the existence of Satan and demons, a non-eternal universe, and the hidden meanings of Scripture. For Origen, these elements were to be included with the essential teachings of the Church.

[54] Kelly uses the terminology "arch-heretic" which displays the lasting effect of Arius's influence on theological discourse. All other heretics are often compared to him. See Kelly, *Early Christian Doctrine*, 223.

[55] Dünzl, *Short History*, 43.

[56] Kelly, *Early Christian Doctrine*, 227.

God could not have a beginning or be divided, Arius viewed Jesus as a separate created being.

Tracing the fragmented evidence of Arius's writings rebuilt from Athanasius' refutation of his view, Kelly has summarized Arius's proposition regarding the nature of the Son in four propositions. First, the Son of God must be a creature created by God out of nothing but God's own decree. The Son is a perfect being and above all of creation but not on the same level as God in substance or essence. Second, the Son as a creature had a beginning. Third, the Son does not have direct communion with the Father. He is entirely distinct from the Father. And fourth, various passages imply ignorance or weakness on part of the Son. Arius appealed to these passages, feeling that ignorance and weakness displayed distinction and separation from Father.[57] Arius still spoke of a Holy Triad but he viewed them as distinct persons, grounding much of his thought on an extreme Origenistic interpretation. Kelly notes that the net result of Arius' teaching was to reduce Jesus, as the Son of God, to a demigod.[58]

As Alexander's assistant and then later becoming the Bishop of Alexandria in his place, Athanasius strongly opposed the teaching of Arius. In *On the Incarnation of the Word*, he firmly asserted, "The Word of the Father is Himself divine, that all things that are owe their being to His will and power, and that it is through Him that the Father gives order to creation, by Him that all things are moved, and through Him that they receive their being."[59] For Athanasius, Jesus was not a created being but was one with the Father in substance. The true divinity of the Son along with his incarnational oneness with humanity provided the necessary foundation for the soteriological work of Christ.

Athanasius further stated, "For He alone, being Word of the Father and above all, was in consequence both able to recreate all, and worthy to suffer on behalf of all and to be an ambassador for all with the Father."[60] Athanasius stressed that Arius' teaching of the subordinate nature of the Son as a created being drastically affected the efficacy of Jesus' sacrifice on the cross. In Athanasius's view, Arius's teaching was wrong not because it did not match his own but because it did not match the very narrative of Scripture regarding the nature of Jesus.

Although Arius's teaching was met with strong opposition and condemnation from Alexander and Athanasius, Arius was able to garner a few powerful followers. Far from derailing the development of the doctrine of Trinity, though, the Arian controversy can be seen as an important step in

---

[57] All four points are drawn from Kelly, *Early Christian Doctrines*, 229–30.

[58] Ibid., 230.

[59] Athanasius, *On the Incarnation of the Word*, 1.1; trans. accessed at https://www.ccel.org/ccel/athanasius/incarnation.ii.html.

[60] Ibid., 2.7.

identifying the essential characteristics of the doctrine. Pelikan astutely notes that in many ways Arian thought was more aware of the complexity and "nuances of the Trinitarian problem" than the opposition.[61] The Arian controversy forced the theological discourse to be more precise, to avoid oversimplification, and to guard itself against heretical leanings in the other direction. Pelikan notes, "As the official doctrine of the church proceeded to settle the question of the relation of Christ to God by means of the formula 'homoousios,' it was Arianism that helped, through its demand for precision, to rescue the formula from the heretical, Gnostic incubus that afflicted it."[62]

Greater precision and clarity forced by the Arian controversy was produced at the Council of Nicaea in the form of a strong creedal statement. Evident in the stanzas of the Nicene Creed is a clear condemnation of Arian thought and at the same time a clear positive statement regarding the nature of Trinitarian thought:

> We believe in one God, the Father Almighty, Maker of all things, visible and invisible; And in one Lord Jesus Christ, the Son of God, begotten from the Father, light from light, true God from true God, begotten not made, of one substance with the Father.[63]

The creed developed at the Council of Nicaea, while developing a strong Christology, produced only a short stanza on the Holy Spirit, leaving further room for clarity and precision in terms of the entire Trinity. Kelly notes that the theology of the council had a more limited objective in terms of denouncing Arianism and affirming the full divinity and coequality of the Son, as evidenced by its brevity in regards to the Spirit.[64] While the Nicene Creed was a major advancement in the theological discourse concerning the Trinity it did not signify, as Pelikan notes, "theological unanimity."[65] Church leaders wrestled with understanding and supporting the main tenets of the creed for over a half century until it was ratified and expanded by the Council of Constantinople in 381.

Cappadocian Fathers

In the heart of this developmental period between the Councils of Nicaea and Constantinople lies the strong voices of the Cappadocian Fathers: Basil of Caesarea (c. AD 330–379), Gregory of Nazianzus (c. AD 330–389), Gregory of Nyssa (c. AD 335–394?), and Amphilochius of Iconium (AD

---

[61] Pelikan, *Christian Tradition*, 200.
[62] Ibid.
[63] This text is drawn from Schaff, *Creeds of Christendom*, 28–29.
[64] Kelly, *Early Christian Doctrine*, 236.
[65] Pelikan, *Christian Tradition*, 203.

340–345?).[66] Basil, in his treatise *On the Holy Spirit*, examined the theology of the Holy Spirit bringing a particular focus on the Spirit that was not fully developed by his earlier Patristic predecessors. In reaction to any form of Sabellian understanding of the Trinity, which was not "solved" with the first iteration of the Nicene Creed, John Zizioulas notes that the Cappadocian Fathers stressed the "ontological integrity" of each person of the Holy Triad.

Zizioulas asserts that they did this by identifying the term *hypostasis* with *prosopon* (person) instead of *ousia* (substance).[67] Justo Gonzalez notes that the Cappadocian Fathers aided in "clarifying, defining, and defending Trinitarian doctrine . . . expounding it with as much logical clarity as possible."[68] Olsen notes that their main object was to "explain the Trinity in a way that clearly distinguished it from these heresies and protected the mystery at its heart without leaving it as a sheer contradiction."[69]

The Cappadocian Fathers' work led to a revision of the creed formulated at Nicaea in 325 and a deeper understanding of the logic of Trinitarian thought. This revision is reflected in key edits like the change of the phrase "from the substance of the Father" found in the first Nicene Creed to simply "from the Father." One also notes the additional description given to the Holy Spirit. The first creed included only one phrase "We believe in the Holy Spirit," but the revised version expanded it to, "We believe in the Holy Spirit, the Lord, and giver of life, who proceeds from the Father, Who with the Father and the Son together is worshipped and glorified, Who spoke by the Prophets."[70]

This final formulation of the great Creed that is recited today did not end the theological discussion concerning the Trinity, though. Rather it provides a starting place for further discourse and further development, in the spirit of the Cappadocian Fathers, of the complexity of such a grand doctrine.

---

[66] John D. Zizioulas, "The Doctrine of the Holy Trinity: The Significance of the Cappadocian Contribution," in *Trinitarian Theology Today: Essays on Divine Being and Act*, ed. by Christoph Schwöbel (Edinburgh: T & T Clark, 1995), 44. Zizioulas denotes uncertainty in the dates for some of the Fathers by using the question mark.

[67] Zizioulas, "Doctrine of the Holy Trinity," 45.

[68] Justo L. Gonzalez, *A History of Christian Thought*, Rev ed., vol. I (Nashville, TN: Abingdon Press, 1993), 300.

[69] Olsen, *The Story of Christian Theology*, 175.

[70] It should be noted here that the *filioque* clause is added in 589 by Western churches after the Synod of Toledo and is controversial for the church in the East because for them it disregards the Father as the single origin and source of the Spirit.

Summary of the Biblical Foundation of the Doctrines

In tracing the theological discourse concerning the doctrines of Christology and the Trinity from the apostolic period to Constantinople, it should have become clear that the church fathers of this time were driven by alignment with the biblical narrative. Irenaeus displayed this as he worked to bring Justin Martyr's teaching into alignment with the full revelation of God found in the biblical narrative.

As noted in the previous section, the various renditions of the Rule of Faith that guided and shaped the theology of the early Patristics were summaries of the essential elements of the biblical narrative and apostolic teachings that had been handed down through tradition. Greenslade notes, in his translation of early Latin fathers, that the Rule was almost "instinctively" drawn from Scripture and apostolic teaching and preserved in the tradition handed down through the writings of the Fathers.[71] This section will provide a summary of the biblical narrative concerning the key elements of Scripture that guided this early theological discourse.[72]

In contrast to other religious narratives, the biblical narrative, from the Hebrew Bible to the New Testament, boldly proclaims that there is only one true God. The Shema, as noted in the previous chapter, states, "Hear, O Israel: The Lord is our God, the Lord alone. You shall love the Lord your God with all your heart, and with all your soul, and with all your might" (Deut 6:4–5). Bird notes that as these words were confessed daily by faithful Jews, they served to distinguish themselves from the pagan polytheists who surrounded them. In Exodus one finds a similar proclamation in the song of Moses, who in retelling the story of their salvation from slavery in Egypt sings,

> Who is like you, O Lord, among the gods?
> Who is like you, majestic in holiness,
> awesome in splendor, doing wonders? (Ex 15:11)

At the dedication of the Temple, Solomon prays "that all the peoples of the earth may know that the Lord is God; there is no other" (1 Kgs 8:60).

---

[71] S. L. Greenslade, ed., *Early Latin Theology: Selections from Tertullian, Cyprian, Ambrose, and Jerome* (Philadelphia, PA: Westminster Press, 1978), 40.

[72] This section is located after the survey of the theological discourse leading up to the councils in order to reinforce that the essential identity markers identified and articulated by the conciliar creeds were indeed drawn from Scripture and not mere theological inventions. Subsequent case studies will also follow this structure.

Wayne Grudem notes that when God speaks, God often stresses that God is the one true God,[73] as seen in God speaking through the prophet Isaiah:

> I am the Lord, and there is no other;
>> besides me there is no god.
>> I arm you, though you do not know me,
> so that they may know, from the rising of the sun
>> and from the west, that there is no one besides me;
>> I am the Lord, and there is no other (Isa 45:5–6)

And again in verses 21–22,

> Declare and present your case;
>> let them take counsel together!
> Who told this long ago?
>> Who declared it of old?
> Was it not I, the Lord?
>> There is no other god besides me,
> a righteous God and a Savior;
>> there is no one besides me.
> Turn to me and be saved,
>> all the ends of the earth!
>> For I am God, and there is no other.

God presents Godself as completely unique, with no rivals or counterparts. God alone is worthy of praise, and God alone is the savior of God's people.

These statements found in the Hebrew Bible form the foundation for the strong monotheism of the Jewish religion. They also serve to guide the doctrine of God in Christian theology. As noted in the previous section, Irenaeus, Tertullian, and Origen all highlighted the biblical narrative's affirmation of this oneness of God in their renditions of the Rule of Faith. The New Testament also carries on this theme of the oneness of God. James, in proving a point on faith and action, notes that even demons believe that "God is one" (Jas 2:19). Paul also stresses that God is one (see Rom 3:30) but often Paul provided a twist that opens the conversation to further exploration. Often when Paul affirmed the oneness of God he also includes Jesus.

In his first letter to Timothy, Paul noted, "For there is one God; there is also one mediator between God and humankind, Christ Jesus,

---

[73] Wayne A. Grudem, *Systematic Theology: An Introduction to Biblical Doctrine* (Leicester, England: Inter-Varsity Press, 1994), 238.

himself human" (1 Tim 2:5). Paul makes this connection again in 1 Cor 8:6, "Yet for us there is one God, the Father, from whom are all things and for whom we exist, and one Lord, Jesus Christ, through whom are all things and through whom we exist." The juxtaposition of one God and one Lord Jesus in Paul's writings provides an intriguing turn in the biblical narrative concerning the oneness of God. Luke Timothy Johnson notes that Paul here appears to be expanding the Shema to include Jesus, a bold move in terms of the strict monotheism of Judaism.[74]

The identification of Jesus with YHWH in the biblical narrative underscores the effect of Christological claims on the formation of Trinitarian thought and brings in the entire biblical narrative concerning the nature of Jesus. In the narrative of the New Testament one sees several claims made about Jesus and some made by himself, which begin to shade theology's understanding of the relationship between the Son and the Father. The first chapter of John's Gospel begins with the poetic and strikingly clear claim, "In the beginning was the Word, and the Word was with God, and the Word was God" (John 1:1).[75] One also sees the stronger claims of the primitive Christian tradition in the writings of Paul, specifically in his letter to the Philippians. This study has already noted the creedal nature of Phil 2:6–11 and the claim it makes of the divinity of Jesus as seen in the phrase "equality with God" (Phil 2:6). Millard Erikson stresses that Paul's statement here, or reference to an earlier tradition, stands as an "astonishing statement" in light of his orthodox Jewish training.[76]

Erickson also notes that Jesus' view of himself as presented in the Synoptic Gospels displays a strong connection with the Father for he claims to possess what traditionally belongs to God. "He spoke of the angels of God (Luke 12:8–9; 15:10) as his angels (Matt 13:41). He regards the kingdom of God (Matt 12:28; 19:14, 24; 21:31, 43) and the elect of God (Mark 13:20) as his own."[77] He also claims to be able to do what only God can do regarding the forgiveness of sins (Mark 2:8–10). The reactions of the scribes in this passage shows the full weight of Jesus's claim. Their consideration of his claim as blasphemy indicates that Jesus was claiming much more than just a special status with the Father.

In the same way, Brevard Childs notes that Jesus is attributed other titles and functions of YHWH in the New Testament: Jesus sits in YHWH's judgment seat in 1 Cor 5:10; he is worshipped by all (Phil 2:10, c.f. Isa

---

[74] Johnson, *Creed*, 12.

[75] While modern scholarship is somewhat skeptical of the high Christology found in John's Gospel, the early Church Fathers do not show any signs of skepticism and were guided by John's writings as much as Paul's.

[76] Millard J. Erickson, *Christian Theology* (Grand Rapids, MI: Baker Book House, 1998), 350.

[77] Ibid., 351.

45:23), Jesus's return is associated with the Day of the Lord from the Hebrew Bible (1 Thess 5:2); and even Angels worship him (Heb 1:6; Rev 5:13).[78] Horton asserts that perhaps no stronger claim to the divinity of Christ could be made than the proclamation by "the apostles that there is no other name in heaven or on earth by which we may be saved (John 1:12; Acts 3:16; 4:12; 5:41; Rom 10:13; Phil 2:9; 1 Pet 4:14; Rev 2:13)."[79] Here the apostles are clearly identifying Jesus with Israel's savior YHWH.

In terms of Trinitarian thought, the biblical narrative also introduces a third character with the Father and the Son, the Holy Spirit, who is presented as a distinct person along with the Father and the Son. Both in Acts 5:3–4 and 1 Cor 3:16–17, the Holy Spirit and God are referenced interchangeably. The Holy Spirit performs personal acts like conviction of sin (John 16:8–11), regeneration (John 3:8), and giving gifts to the church (1 Cor 12:4–11). Grudem notes that the term *paraklētos* given the Spirit (John 14:16, 26; 15:26; 16:7) is used to denote a person who gives counsel and comfort.[80] The Holy Spirit is also related with the Father and the Son who are both distinct persons (Matt 28:19; 1 Cor 12:4–6; 2 Cor 13:14; Eph 4:4–6; 1 Pet 1:2).

None of the biblical passages referenced in this section alone serve as "proof texts" for the doctrine of the Trinity. When taken together, though, they serve as regulative guides in the development of the unique Christian identity of the doctrine. They provide the proper parameters that guided the theological discourse of the first three centuries of Christian thought leading up to the church councils and formulated creeds of the fourth century.

As has been noted already, the councils and formalized creeds did not end the great theological discourse of the church, but they did give shape to it. All other discourse should understand and explore the implications of the findings stated in the creeds, which in turn were formalized summaries of the biblical narrative. The next section will briefly survey seven theological voices from the fifth century to the present to examine the influence of creedal affirmations as essential identity markers on further development of the doctrine of the Trinity.

---

[78] Brevard S. Childs, *Biblical Theology of the Old and New Testaments: Theological Reflection on the Christian Bible* (Minneapolis, MN: Fortress Press, 1993), 363–64. See also Michael Scott Horton, *The Christian Faith: A Systematic Theology for Pilgrims on the Way* (Grand Rapids, MI: Zondervan, 2011), 276.

[79] Horton, *Christian Faith*, 277.

[80] Grudem, *Systematic Theology*, 232.

Brief Survey of Seven Theological Voices (Fifth Century – Present)

The starting point for this survey will be the Pro-Nicene and Cappadocian emphasis that God is one nature (*ousia*) and three persons (*hypostases*). This section will particularly examine how seven key theologians built upon the essential identity markers solidified by the creeds. These seven have been chosen for their contributions in furthering Trinitarian and Christological theological discourse and their understanding of the role of creedal affirmations in guiding such discourse.

Augustine (AD 354–430)

Augustine emerges as a key voice regarding the development of the doctrine of the Trinity not long after the Council of Constantinople, writing *De Trinitate* over a twenty-year period early in the fifth century. In his work, Augustine took on the task of further defending the doctrine of the Trinity from various Arian and Sabellian heresies with a particular focus on the former. Robert Thom notes that Augustine sought to demonstrate the "logical consistency" of the doctrine, using an Aristotelian-based theory of categories.[81] Thom also notes that Augustine further developed the notion of substance, favoring *essentia* over *substantia*.[82] In *De Trinitate*, Augustine wrote, "There is at least no doubt that God is substance, or perhaps a better word would be being; at any rate what the Greeks call *ousia*."[83]

   While Augustine stressed the unity and equality of the Godhead against any form of subordinationism, Alister McGrath notes that Augustine makes a key development in understanding the difference between the eternal Godhead and their roles in the work of salvation, a point that will shape the later theological development of the immanent and economic Trinity.[84] Augustine noted that there was a difference regarding God's unity and coequality in essence and in the way each person is revealed in history and the continued the work of salvation. Thom notes that Augustine's view can be summarized as an affirmation of "a single substance and three relatives, in which, while distinct from each other in their relativities, are all substantially identical."[85]

   It is clear from Augustine's writings that his theological development built upon prior creedal formulations. In his work *On Faith*

---

   [81] Paul Thom, *The Logic of the Trinity: Augustine to Ockham* (New York: Fordham University Press, 2012), 21.

   [82] Ibid., 25.

   [83] Augustine, *De Trinitate* 5.2:1–2.

   [84] Alister E. McGrath, *Christian Theology: An Introduction*, 3rd ed. (Oxford, UK: Blackwell Publishers, 2001), 332.

   [85] Thom, *Logic of the Trinity*, 32.

and the Creed, he most explicitly notes this connection. *On Faith and the Creed* is a revision of an address given by Augustine to the full assembly of leaders of the church in North Africa in 393. The work marks Augustine's first commentary concerning prior creedal formulations.

Finbarr Glancy notes that "while a Latin translation of the Nicene Creed had been submitted for approval at this council, Augustine's commentary is based on an amalgam of the Nicene and Romano-Milanese creeds, not precisely in the form given to catechumens."[86] In the work, Augustine explored the Trinitarian framework that is captured in the creed and particularly stresses the consubstantiality with the Father of both the Son and the Spirit against any competing claims. Concerning the second article of the creed concerning Jesus Christ as the only-begotten Son of God, Augustine noted,

> By this catholic faith, therefore, those are excluded, on the one hand, who affirm that the Son is the same [Person] as the Father; for [it is clear that] this Word could not possibly be *with* God, were it not with God *the Father*, and [it is just as evident that] He who is *alone* is *equal* to no one. And, on the other hand, those are equally excluded who affirm that the Son is a creature, although not such an one as the rest of the creatures are.[87]

Augustine understood the Creed as containing the universal faith of the church. In *Sermon 213*, Augustine assures a group of baptismal candidates that the creed summarizes the Rule of Faith that had been drawn from Scripture and passed down through the apostolic tradition.[88] Augustine was not content in merely reaffirming the tenets of the creed, though, and clearly probes deeper into the meanings and implications of these essential points.

Boethius (c. AD 475–526)

Boethius has been long recognized and celebrated as a bridge between the Greek and Latin philosophies of the early church and the Latin Middle Ages. His work lays the foundation for later theologians like Aquinas and displays the interweaving of philosophy and theology as seen in Augustine. Boethius

---

[86] Finbarr G. Glancy, "Fide et symbolo, De," in *Augustine through the Ages: An Encyclopedia*, edited by Allan Fitzgerald and John C. Cavadini (Grand Rapids, MI: W.B. Eerdmans, 1999), 360.

[87] Augustine *On Faith and the Creed* 4.5; trans. *NPNF* 1–3.

[88] See Lewis Ayres, "Augustine on the Rule of Faith: Rhetoric, Christology, and the Foundation of Christian Thinking," *Augustinian Studies* 36, no. 1 (2005): 35, for keen insight on this sermon.

affirmed the Nicene understanding of the Trinity and appealed to Augustine's understanding of the relativeness of the persons of the Trinity:

> The manifoldness of the Trinity is secured through the category of relation, and the Unity is maintained through the fact that there is no difference of substance, or operation, or generally of any substantial predicate. So, then, the divine substance preserves the Unity, the divine relations bring about the Trinity.[89]

Thom notes that, much like Augustine, Boethius framed his understanding of the Trinity within a modified Aristotelian theory of categories.[90] Boethius explored the category of relation a bit further to note that while the persons of the Trinity are of one substance they are not identical. Further, their distinction is to be seen only in relation to each other: "Father and son are predicates of relation, and, as we have said, have no other difference but that of relation."[91] Ultimately, in order to understand their unity and threeness, Boethius appealed to the different relativities of Father, Son, and Spirit within the one God.

In his theological treatise *On the Catholic Faith*, Boethius affirmed the essential identity markers noted in the creedal faith of the church and connected them with the teachings of both the Hebrew Bible and the New Testament.[92] Concerning the church's teaching on the Trinity, Boethius noted,

> From all eternity, that is, before the world was established, and so before all that is meant by time began, there has existed one divine substance of Father, Son, and Holy Spirit in such wise that we confess the Father God, the Son God, and the Holy Spirit God, and yet not three Gods but one God.[93]

Boethius used this foundational teaching of the church as a guide for his own theological explorations in the rest of the treatise. Here Boethius allowed the creedal framework to guide and shape his theology.

---

[89] Boethius *OS I, De Trinitate*, I.6:1–9.
[90] Thom, *Logic of the Trinity*, 50.
[91] Boethius I.5:33–40.
[92] See *On the Catholic Faith*; trans. accessed at http://www.ccel.org/ccel/boethius/tracts.iv.iv.html.
[93] Ibid.

Thomas Aquinas (1225–1274)

The grand theological work of Thomas Aquinas reflects the theology and philosophy of both Augustine and Boethius. Much like Augustine and Boethius, Aquinas understood the simplicity of God as a fundamental attribute of God's essence. "In God, therefore, we posit substance and being—substance by reason of subsisting not by reason of sub-standing, but being by reason of simplicity and completeness not by reason of an inherence by which it inheres in another."[94] For Aquinas, the simplicity of God serves as the foundation for understanding the three persons of the Godhead. Aquinas followed Boethius in understanding the distinction of the three persons in terms of relationship within God.

Thom notes that for Aquinas these relations within God are not merely conceptual, but rather they are a part of the divine essence.[95] The Father, Son, and Spirit exist in relation to one another in one essence eternally. In many ways, Aquinas's work stands as the climax of the philosophical theology of the scholastic period and stands as an affirmation of the creedal theology of the Trinity with further exploration of the philosophical foundations of it.

In his work *Expositio in Symbolum Apostolorum*, Aquinas probed the key tenets of creedal faith laid out in the Apostles' Creed. In his exploration, Aquinas unpacks the Trinitarian reality expounded by the Creed. Commenting on the second article of the Creed, Aquinas noted, "It is not only necessary for Christians to believe in one God who is the Creator of heaven and earth and of all things; but also they must believe that God is the Father and that Christ is the true Son of God."[96] Aquinas proceeded to refute the heresies of Photinus, Sabellius, and Arius in light of this understanding of the second article.

Regarding the Holy Spirit, Aquinas noted that in order to fend off heretical teaching the Fathers added more depth in the Nicene Creed to the proclamation of faith asserted in the Apostles' Creed.[97] Aquinas then highlighted the benefits of affirming belief in the Holy Spirit as a part of the Holy Trinity. Here one notes the creedal nature of Aquinas's theology and also his ability to probe deeper into the meaning and implications of the great claims of the early creeds.

---

[94] Thomas Aquinas, *De Potentia* 1.1.

[95] Thom, *Logic of the Trinity*, 136.

[96] Thomas Aquinas, *Expositio Symbolum Apostolorum* Article 2, paragraph 1; trans. John B. Collins, 1939, accessed at http://dhspriory.org/thomas/Creed.htm#1.

[97] Ibid., Article 8, paragraph 2.

John Calvin (1509–1564)

John Calvin, along with other major theologians of the Reformation, affirmed the Patristic understanding of the doctrine of the Trinity, three *hypostases* in one *ousia*, without exception. In fact, as Stephen Holmes notes that the 1536 version of his *Institutes* deals with the doctrine of the Trinity only briefly, and not until he is charged with Arianism by his critics does he explores the doctrine in much more depth.[98] While Calvin struggled with the manmade aspects of the doctrine, ultimately his acceptance of the patristic understanding of the doctrine was based on the underlying reformation cry of *sola scriptura*.[99] For Calvin, the patristic understanding of the doctrine effectively expresses what is revealed about the nature of God in Holy Scripture.[100] In the later editions of the *Institutes*, Calvin focused on the biblical evidence of the full divinity of the Son and the Spirit to further support the traditional doctrine of the Trinity. Here Calvin further developed the doctrine by stressing divinity is not derived from the Father and gifted to the Son and the Spirit but rather is possessed eternally by all three with aseity.

One cannot fully understand Calvin's theology without understanding the way in which Augustine influenced him. In his *Institutes*, Calvin quotes extensively from Augustine's writings. Francois Wendel notes that in-depth study of Augustine allowed Calvin to quote him so extensively, often using him to support and verify his own theological understanding of Scripture.[101] In detailing his own theological method Calvin noted,

> Let us undertake to summarize the matter for our readers by but a few, and very clear, testimonies of Scripture. Then, lest anyone accuse us of distorting Scripture, let us show that the truth, which we assert has been drawn from Scripture, lacks not the attestation of this holy man—I mean Augustine.[102]

---

[98] Stephen R. Holmes, *The Quest for the Trinity: The Doctrine of God in Scripture, History, and Modernity* (Downers Grove, IL: IVP Academic, 2012), 168.

[99] In the opening sections of his chapter on the Trinity in the *Institutes*, Calvin did wrestle with the use of nonbiblical terms like *homoousia*, person, and trinity, but ultimately supported them as they sufficiently express the biblical revelation.

[100] Stephen Reynolds does note, though, that Calvin was hesitant in proclaiming the formal creeds in lieu of the biblical record not wanting to put more weight in the words of men over God. See Stephen M. Reynolds, "Calvin's View of the Athanasian and Nicene Creeds," *Westminster Theological Journal* 23, no. 1 (November 1960): 34.

[101] Francois Wendel, *Calvin: The Origins and Development of His Religious Thought*, trans. Philip Mairet (New York: Harper & Row, 1963), 124.

[102] John Calvin, *Institutes of the Christian Religion*, 2.3.8; trans. accessed at http://www.ccel.org/ccel/calvin/institutes.iii.vi.html.

Randall Zachman notes that this exemplifies Calvin's overall theological method, which always begins with biblical support but also uses the testimony of the early Fathers to show that his thought is not novel.[103] Calvin's model here mirrors the creedal process described in this book.

In appealing to the early fathers for support and validation, Calvin placed himself squarely within the orthodox tradition of early Christian thought. Calvin affirmed the authority of the early councils and their polemic work, namely Nicaea in refuting Arius, Constantinople in silencing Eunomius and Macedonius, and the first Council of Ephesus in defeating Nestorius.[104] He denied, though, that all interpretations of Scripture supported by councils, especially later councils, were to be accepted without scrutiny, noting that "all ages and places are not favored with an Athanasius, a Basil, a Cyril, and like vindicators of sound doctrine, whom the Lord then raised up."[105]

Friedrich Schleiermacher (1768–1834)

Known as the father of modern theology, Friedrich Schleiermacher and his theological and philosophical works, *On Religion* and *The Christian Faith*, changed the landscape of nineteenth-century theology. In response to the critiques of religion leveled by the Enlightenment, Schleiermacher emphasized religious experience over historical knowledge.

It is clear from the order of his seminal work, *The Christian Faith*, that the doctrine of the Trinity did not factor as a guide to better understanding the nature of God, for he dealt with it only briefly at the end of the work. For Schleiermacher, the doctrine of the Trinity, which had held fairly the same form from the fourth century to his day, posed too many questions and was open to grave critique. Placing it at the end of his work was an assertion of its unimportance as a foundation for Christian belief and salvation through Christ.[106]

In his brief survey of the doctrine, Schleiermacher struggled with the notion of eternal distinction within the Godhead. William La Due notes that, for Schleiermacher, any distinction within the Godhead leads to subordination and many of the older formulas for noting the Trinity, in Schleiermacher's estimation, lend to this subordination.[107]

---

[103] Randall C. Zachman, *John Calvin as Teacher, Pastor, and Theologian: The Shape of His Writings and Thought* (Grand Rapids, MI: Baker Academic, 2006), 102.

[104] Calvin, *Institutes*, 4.9.13.

[105] Ibid., 4.9.13.

[106] See Friedrich Schleiermacher, *The Christian Faith*, ed. Paul T. Nimmo (New York: Bloomsbury T. & T. Clark, 2016), 754.

[107] William J. La Due, *The Trinity Guide to the Trinity* (Harrisburg, PA: Trinity Press International, 2003), 84.

Schleiermacher noted, "They identify the Father with the unity of the Divine Essence, but not the Son or the Spirit. This can be traced right back to the idea of Origen, that the Father is God absolutely, while the Son and Spirit are God only by participation in the Divine Essence—an idea which is positively rejected by orthodox church teachers, but secretly underlies their whole procedure."[108] While dismissing the importance of the doctrine of the Trinity, Schleiermacher did stress the formation of a strong Christology (though removed from historical referent) and for further evaluation of the old form of the doctrine of the Trinity to make it more intelligible for modernity.

Schleiermacher is included in the discussion here because he serves as an example of a theologian who is not concerned with the essential identity markers set forth by the theological investigation of the early fathers. For him, the ecclesiastical doctrine of the Trinity did not have an immediate effect on his own understanding of Christian identity.[109] This disregard for the creedal process shows a clear line of demarcation regarding the theology leading up to Schleiermacher and the theology to follow.

Karl Barth (1886–1968)

Karl Barth, arguably the most prominent theologian of the twentieth century, in reaction to Schleiermacher and the subjectivity of nineteenth-century German liberalism that followed, elevated the doctrine of the Trinity back to a place of foundational importance. McGrath notes that for Barth, the doctrine of the Trinity "undergirds and guarantees the actuality of divine revelation to sinful humanity."[110] For Barth, the doctrine of the Trinity confirmed the revelation of God as seen in Christ, the Word of God. Bruce McCormack notes that for Barth there is no difference in content of the immanent Trinity and the economic Trinity, or the way in which they are revealed in the story of salvation.[111] What is revealed of God in Christ must be true for God in eternity.

Barth affirmed the creedal formulations underlying orthodox Trinitarian thought and attempted to construct an understanding of the Trinity in light of the identity markers set in the creeds. In his commentary on the Apostles' Creed, he noted that in the early councils and creeds, the

---

[108] Schleiermacher, *Christian Faith*, 747.

[109] Ibid., 747.

[110] McGrath, *Christian Theology*, 334.

[111] Bruce McCormack, "The Lord and Giver of Life: A Barthian Defense of Filioque," in *Rethinking Trinitarian Theology: Disputed Questions and Contemporary Issues in Trinitarian Theology*, edited by Giulio Maspero and Robert J. Wozniak (London: T & T Clark, 2012), 231. McCormack does note, though, that even for Barth this rule is difficult to keep.

church receives the fundamental articles of faith.[112] Barth noted that in affirming belief in God, Jesus Christ, and the Holy Spirit (*in Deum . . . et in Jesum Christum . . . et in Spiritum sanctum*), the creeds provide greater detail regarding the object of faith, namely the God of Christian faith.[113]

While Barth affirmed the early creeds, he did take exception to the use of the term *persons*. For Barth, the term, in light of a modern understanding of it, insinuated too great a distinction and separation within the Godhead. Barth preferred to speak of "three modes of the one being of God,"[114] a point that opened him to a charge of modalism by his critics. Barth is not promoting modalism here, but rather stressing the limitations of terminology in fully expressing the mystery of Trinity. This objection also shows Barth's understanding that the creeds, while providing a firm foundation for the work of dogmatics, must be understood anew and reenvisioned in new and unfolding contexts.

Karl Rahner (1904–1984)

Karl Rahner, the preeminent Catholic theologian of the twentieth century, followed in Barth's footsteps in highlighting the importance of the doctrine of the Trinity and also in understanding the relation between the immanent Trinity and the economic Trinity. For Rahner, the formal proclamations of the church found in the early creeds serve as starting points from which to embark on deeper theological investigation. In his essay "Current Problems in Christology," he observed:

> Work by the theologians and teachers of the church bearing on a reality and a truth revealed by God always ends in an exact formulation. That is natural and necessary. For only in this way is it possible to draw a line of demarcation, excluding heresy and misunderstanding of the divine truth, which can be observed in everyday religious practice. But if the formula is this an end, the result and the victory which brings about simplicity, clarity, the possibility of teaching and doctrinal certainty, then in this victory everything depends on the end also being seen as a beginning.[115]

---

[112] Barth, *Credo*, 3.

[113] Ibid., 2.

[114] Karl Barth, *Church Dogmatics* 1/1, trans. Geoffrey W. Bromiley and Thomas F. Torrance (Edinburgh, Scotland: T & T Clark, 1962), 348.

[115] Karl Rahner, "Current Problems in Christology," in *Theological Investigations.*, vol. 1 (Baltimore, MD: Helicon Press, 1965), 200. The original title of the article in German was "Chalcedon—Ende oder Anfang?"

For Rahner the creeds stand as foundational affirmations of the church and also mark the beginning of further theological study.

Rahner's most famous contribution to the study of the doctrine of the Trinity is his axiom: "The 'economic' Trinity is the 'immanent' Trinity, and the 'immanent' Trinity is the 'economic' Trinity."[116] Here Rahner stressed the relation between how God has been revealed in history and how God exists ontologically. Rahner asserted that the manner in which God reveals Godself corresponds to the manner in which God truly is. God is Trinity. This assertion from Rahner and his reluctance to use the terminology of *persons* has left him, much like Barth, open to the accusation of modalism, though Rahner was emphatic in his defense against the charge. For Rahner, the unity of the essence of God must also be seen in his revelation. God revealed as three implies God is three in one being.

Implications for Teaching the Doctrines Today

The specific doctrines of the Trinity and Christology stand as an excellent case study in understanding the process of theological development as well as the influence of the creedal process that emerged within the first three hundred years of Christianity. This creedal process of identifying and articulating the essential elements of the biblical narrative provides the foundation for the EIM model presented in this book. Applying the EIM model in teaching these doctrines today helps refocus the theological discourse onto the essential claims of the biblical narrative and provides helpful parameters in examining and testing the theories further developed by the Christian community.

As the brief survey of theological voices in the last section displayed, the conversation evolved from parameters set in the creeds to a deeper exploration of *how* the doctrine works. This further development is vitally important for theological discourse but can also leave the student of theology lost in a sea of contrasting voices, without a clear grasp on what the essentials are and how they guide the conversation. The EIM model reestablishes the essential markers presented in the biblical narrative and articulated by church.

As noted in this chapter, at least three essential identity markers emerge in regard to the doctrine of the Trinity: (1) there is only one God; (2) Jesus Christ, the Son of God, and the Holy Spirit, along with God the Father, are each fully God; and (3) the three are distinct persons. From the Shema to the pages of the New Testament, God is clearly presented and worshiped as one, but Jesus and the Holy Spirit are also identified with this one God and given full deity in person and action. Each person is also clearly expressed

---

[116] Karl Rahner, *The Trinity* (New York: Burnes & Oates, 2001), 21.

as distinct from the other. This unity and plurality captures the tension that sketches the particularly Christian identity of God. The EIM model seeks to rearticulate these claims and reemphasize their vitality in guiding theological discourse.

The early Christian creeds express this triadic formula without much further development. They simply note the essential Christian elements of the biblical narrative, the *what* of Scripture. Later theological voices take up the work of explaining and understanding the *how*. How does one understand (and defend) the three-in-one nature of God? From the Cappadocian Fathers to Augustine, to Barth and Rahner, the conversation moves to the *how*. The EIM model notes the importance of this further discourse but also notes its limitations and speculative nature. Discussion of the *how*, as in the various analogous models of the Trinity, often falls short of fully grasping each essential element of the Christian identity. Rearticulating the essential identity markers provides the student of theology with the proper tools of assessing further theological discourse concerning the doctrine.

Further theological development, though, can also help the student of theology reunderstand or reenvision particular articulations of the EIMs. Barth's and Rahner's aversion to using the term *person* highlights how changes in language can affect how one expresses the EIMs drawn from the biblical narrative. Much like the creeds themselves, EIMs drawn from the biblical narrative do not stand as untouchable axioms but rather guides in exploring the depths of God's revelation.

3

Case Study 2 — Creation in the Creeds

Along with the doctrines of the Trinity and Christology, the doctrine of creation stands as a foundational doctrine for developing a deeper understanding of the unique Christian identity laid out in the core narrative of Scripture. Both the Apostles' and Nicene Creeds open by emphatically affirming belief in God as creator. The Apostles' Creed simply states, "I believe in God the Father almighty, creator of heaven and earth."[1] The Nicene Creed elaborates: "We believe in one God, the Father Almighty, Maker of heaven and earth, and of all things visible and invisible."[2] John Zizioulas notes that the reference to the creative work of God in these creeds stands as an addition to the primitive baptismal confessions of the church in order to clearly distinguish the God of Christianity from heretical claims emerging in the second and third centuries.[3]

Likewise, Kelly asserts that the declaration of God as creator by the early church fathers connected the Christian faith with its Jewish roots and also "marked the dividing line between the Church and paganism."[4] The God professed by the Christian faith was the creator YHWH of Israel, the creator of all things and therefore above all things. The declaration of God as creator also affirmed the intrinsic value of creation itself.

This chapter will follow the structure laid out in the previous case study concerning the doctrines of the Trinity and Christology. First it will trace the theological development of the doctrine of creation from creedal formulations found in the biblical text through the later apostolic and patristic periods leading up Constantinople, paying particular attention to the influence of the various renditions of the Rule of Faith prior to the formalized creeds.

A summary of the primary affirmations of Scripture that shaped this development will be provided before surveying several key theological

---

[1] Drawn from the text in Kelly, *Early Christian Creeds*, 369.

[2] Text drawn from Schaff, *Creeds of* Christendom, 28–29.

[3] John D. Zizioulas, *Lectures in Christian Dogmatics*, ed. Douglas H. Knight (London: T & T Clark, 2008), 83.

[4] Kelly, *Early Christian Doctrines*, 83.

voices that further developed understanding of the doctrine of creation. The chapter will conclude by briefly highlighting a few implications for teaching the doctrine today. Again, the purpose for this case study is to better understand the influence of the creedal process, the process of identifying and articulating essential affirmations of the Christian faith, on theological development in order to construct a theological method that models this process.

Historical Development (Apostolic Period to Constantinople)

While the narrative of the good news of salvation brought to all humanity through the death and resurrection of Jesus served as the theological foundation for the origin of Christian thought, other fundamental claims also served foundational roles in theological development. As noted in the introduction, a fundamental claim of the Triune God in Christian theology is that God is creator. This claim is overwhelmingly grounded and supported in the Hebrew Bible and serves a foundational role in the emergence of Christian theology.

In the book of Acts, a protocreedal statement appears which connects the story of the God of Abraham with Jesus of Nazareth. This protocreedal statement comes from the prayers of the new community of Christians, who are rejoicing along with Peter and John of the spread of the good of Jesus, and simply affirms, "Sovereign Lord, who made the heaven and the earth, the sea, and everything in them" (Acts 4:24).[5] The prayer goes on to align this creator God with the Davidic Messiah and the fulfillment of this promise in the person of Jesus. This simple phrase, "maker of heaven and earth," speaks a resounding claim about *who* the God of Christianity is. This God is the creator God who spoke through the prophets, who rescued the people of Israel time and time again, and who has now sent a final savior into the world.

The Apostle Paul builds upon this foundational claim in his missionary travels as a way of bringing the Jews and Gentiles together in worship and recognition of the same God. Interestingly, he especially uses the same foundational claim in dealing primarily with Gentile audiences. Jewish audiences would have easily understood the idea of God as creator, but Paul does not only appeal to those who would readily accept it rather he uses it to establish unity with Gentile audiences. On his first missionary

---

[5] In this creedal phrase, one sees the echoes of Psalm 95:3–5, "For the Lord is a great God, and a great King above all gods. In his hand are the depths of the earth; the heights of the mountains are his also. The sea is his, for he made it, and the dry land, which his hands have formed." And Psalm 100:3, "Know that the Lord is God. It is he that made us, and we are his; we are his people, and the sheep of his pasture."

travels through the Galatian region, after those in Lystra began to worship both Paul and Barnabas, Paul asserted:

> Friends, why are you doing this? We are mortals just like you, and we bring you good news, that you should turn from these worthless things to the living God, *who made the heaven and the earth and the sea and all that is in them.* In past generations he allowed all the nations to follow their own ways; yet he has not left himself without a witness in doing good—giving you rains from heaven and fruitful seasons, and filling you with food and your hearts with joy (Acts 14:15–17, emphasis added).

Here the same protocreedal phrase as noted earlier appears: "who made the heaven and the earth and the sea and all that is in them." Paul emphasized to the people of Lystra that the God who made everything had a message for them and deserved their praise and adoration. The act of creation places this God above all other gods.

Later in his missionary travels, as he stood before the philosophers of Athens in front of the Areopagus, Paul asserted that the God he proclaimed is the creator of world and all that is in it. In this assertion Paul used one of the idols he saw in the city to proclaim the message of God:

> For as I went through the city and looked carefully at the objects of your worship, I found among them an altar with the inscription, 'To an unknown god.' What therefore you worship as unknown, this I proclaim to you. The God who made the world and everything in it, he who is Lord of heaven and earth, does not live in shrines made by human hands, nor is he served by human hands, as though he needed anything, since he himself gives to all mortals life and breath and all things. From one ancestor he made all nations to inhabit the whole earth, and he allotted the times of their existence and the boundaries of the places where they would live, so that they would search for God and perhaps grope for him and find him—though indeed he is not far from each one of us (Acts 17:23–27).

Again, Paul used the affirmation of God as creator to establish unity with the Athenians as well as to lay a foundation for the good news of Jesus Christ. It is important for the development of this chapter to note that Paul did not simply tell the story of Jesus here but instead appealed to God as creator as the foundational narrative framework within which the story of Jesus fits. Thus, the assertion of God as creator stands as a fundamental claim or essential identity marker of Christian theology from the very beginning of the apostolic period.

Along with Paul, the affirmation of God as creator is seen in other apostolic writing, most notably in the beginning of the Gospel of John:

> In the beginning was the Word, and the Word was with God, and the Word was God. He was in the beginning with God. All things came into being through him, and without him not one thing came into being. What has come into being in him was life, and the life was the light of all people. The light shines in the darkness, and the darkness did not overcome it (John 1:1–5).

John clearly connected the story of Jesus with the story of creation from Genesis, connecting this new revelation of God with the creator God of the Jewish faith. Daniel Boyarin observes that, more than simply a hymn to the Logos, the opening verses of John's Gospel can also be understood as a homiletic midrash of the Genesis creation account.[6] Jesus as the Logos existed before the creation of the world and was involved in the very act of creation. John used this involvement of the Logos in creation to frame a fundamental affirmation of the person and nature of Jesus, again underscoring the importance of the doctrine of creation for other areas of theology.

Paul Blowers notes that these early apostolic and New Testament writings concerning creation were more doxological in nature than doctrinal and did not attempt to "deal systematically with a 'doctrine of creation.'"[7] Blowers asserts that with the development of the various versions of the church's Rule of Faith in the second and third centuries one sees a transition into a greater understanding of the theological force of the claim. He goes on to note:

> The earliest language of Creator and creation in Christian contexts was primarily narrative, confessional, and doxological. Such language was tied primarily to settings of liturgy, sacramental practice, preaching, and catechesis, but it was not without doctrinal and prescriptive clout insofar as it served to anchor Christian identity in certain normative claims about the Creator-God of Israel revealed most fully now in Jesus Christ.[8]

---

[6] Daniel Boyarin, "The Gospel of the Memra: Jewish Binitarianism and the Prologue of John," *Harvard Theological Review* 94 (2001). See also Paul M. Blowers, *Drama of the Divine Economy: Creator and Creation in Early Christian Theology and Piety* (Oxford, UK: Oxford University Press, 2012), 70.

[7] Blowers, *Drama of the Divine Economy*, 67.

[8] Ibid., 67–68.

The various versions of the Rule of Faith clearly show the theological development unfolding within the early church. As noted in the previous chapter, this Rule was drawn from Scripture and was the attempt of the early church fathers to summarize the essential affirmations of Scripture in order to develop and defend the unique identity of Christian thought.

The proclamation that God is the creator stands as a primary "unchanging, absolute truth" found in the various renditions of the Rule of Faith, observes Litfin,[9] This prominence recognizes the claim of God as creator as foundational in developing a unique Christian identity. It will now be helpful for us to survey the development of the doctrine of creation in the ante-Nicene period, especially through the lens of the various renditions of the Rule of Faith, in order to note the importance of the claim of God as creator.

Irenaeus

The second century marked a robust time of identity formation for the Christian faith, especially in light of divergent views emerging during this time. John Behr highlights the central role that Irenaeus played in this formative period, noting that the orthodoxy of Irenaeus followed Paul's Christocentric understanding of the Christian narrative which extends from the Hebrew Bible into the New Testament.[10] In connecting the story of Jesus with the story of the Hebrew Bible, Irenaeus brought together the two concepts of creation and redemption to identify a genuine Christian metanarrative.

Litfin notes that "the Rule of Faith articulated for Irenaeus a world-encompassing metanarrative" that unified the Christian story.[11] Blowers also notes that Irenaeus aligns the Rule of Faith with the "overarching rhetorical 'argument'...or storyline of Scripture."[12] It is clear from Irenaeus's appeal to the Rule of Faith that his theology and apologetics were guided by the foundational elements drawn from the apostolic tradition which in turn was grounded in Scripture. Blowers observes that the Rule even provided a framework for interpreting Scripture in "its whole and its parts."[13]

In Irenaeus's appeal to the Rule, one clearly sees the affirmation of God as creator as primary and foundational. In the opening line, Irenaeus noted that the Christian tradition believes "in one God, the Creator of heaven

---

[9] Litfin, "Learning," under "2462."

[10] John Behr, *Irenaeus of Lyons: Identifying Christianity* (Oxford, UK: Oxford University Press, 2013), 1.

[11] Litfin, under "2271."

[12] Blowers, *Drama of the Divine Economy*, 76.

[13] Ibid.

and earth."[14] He proceeded to connect this act of creation with Jesus. For Irenaeus, this one Creator God created all things through Jesus Christ.

Blowers observes that "the affirmation of divine creation of the world—more specifically the Father creating through the Logos or Son—appears in most renditions of the Rule as properly basic to Christian belief."[15] For Irenaeus, the affirmation that God created the world and all that it is in it through the Logos was foundational in his apologetic work against various Gnostic and Marcionite heresies. In Book II of *Against Heresies*, Irenaeus strongly proclaimed,

> It is proper, then, that I should begin with the first and most important head, that is, God the Creator, who made the heavens and the earth, and all things that are therein (whom these men blasphemously style the fruit of a defect), and to demonstrate that there is nothing either above Him or after Him; nor that, influenced by any one, but of His own free will, He created all things, since He is the only God, the only Lord, the only Creator, the only Father, alone containing all things, and Himself commanding all things into existence.[16]

Far from being the result of a disinterested, or worse, sinister demiurge, the present world is the creative act of the Father and the Son. For Irenaeus, this creative act is also connected with the redemptive act of God. Here stands Irenaeus's famed theological principle of recapitulation. With this principle, Irenaeus noted that the redemptive work of Jesus Christ was not reactionary in light of humanity's fall, but rather a part of the divine strategy of creation, redemption and consummation. Blowers notes that Irenaeus's doctrine of recapitulation became the standard understanding of the pre-Nicene doctrine of creation because it integrated the work of Christ for salvation and the creative work of the Godhead.[17]

While Irenaeus's doctrine of creation was shaped by the Rule of Faith and the simple proclamation of God as creator of heaven and earth, one also sees further development in Irenaeus's thought in terms of the implications of this proclamation. One further development in the doctrine of creation that Irenaeus shaped is the affirmation that God created the world out of nothing or ex nihilo. John Zizioulas notes that this affirmation stood in opposition to the Platonic idea that the world was eternal, a common belief among the Greeks in the second century.[18]

---

[14] *Against Heresies* 3.4.2.

[15] Blowers, *Drama of the Divine Economy*, 76.

[16] *Against Heresies* 2.1.1. See also, *Demonstration of Apostolic Preaching*, 4.

[17] Blowers, *Drama of the Divine Economy*, 89.

[18] Zizioulas, *Lectures in Christian Dogmatics*, 88–89.

Kelly states that Irenaeus's strong support of creation ex nihilo affirmed the superior nature of God in respect to created beings.[19] Irenaeus stressed, "While men, indeed, cannot make anything out of nothing, but only out of matter already existing, yet God is in this point pre-eminently superior to men, that He Himself called into being the substance of His creation, when previously it had no existence."[20] Irenaeus stressed creation ex nihilo as the necessary understanding of the creedal phrase "creator of heaven and earth," which denoted all things in between.

Tertullian

Tertullian carried on the foundational claim of God as creator much in the same spirit as Irenaeus. Tertullian's own rendition of the Rule of Faith prominently proclaimed God as creator of heaven and earth along with the other core claims of the person and work of Jesus. Litfin notes that for Tertullian, just as with Irenaeus, the Rule formed a "cosmic Christian metanarrative."[21] Litfin also notes that Tertullian used the Rule as an apologetic device in a slightly more advanced way than Irenaeus.

By comparing the narrative laid out by heretical claims with the Rule, Tertullian was able to show that the heretical narrative was not in alignment with the biblical narrative from which the Rule was drawn.[22] In one example, Tertullian attacked those narratives that present Jesus as a mere angelic figure. Using Wisdom's presence at creation, he noted that Jesus was with the Father at the creation of all things. Therefore, Jesus himself was uncreated being connected with the Father:

> How is it that these heretics assume their position so perversely, as to render inadmissible the singleness of that Wisdom which says, "When He prepared the heaven, I was present with Him?"—even though the apostle asks, "Who hath known the mind of the Lord, or who hath been His counsellor?" meaning, of course, to except that wisdom which was present with Him. In Him, at any rate, and with Him, did (Wisdom) construct the universe, He not being ignorant of what she was making. "Except Wisdom," however, is a phrase of the same sense exactly as 'except the Son,' who is Christ, "the Wisdom and Power of God," according to the apostle, who only knows the mind of the Father.[23]

---

[19] Kelly, *Early Christian Doctrines*, 86.
[20] *Against Heresies* 2.10.4.
[21] Litfin, "Learning," under "2283."
[22] Ibid., 2294.
[23] *Against Praxeas*, 18.1; trans. *ANF03*.

For Tertullian, belief could not be held in the heretical narratives that emerged in his time because they simply did not match the biblical narrative. Here one also sees how Tertullian used the doctrine of creation to ground and support the doctrine of the Holy Trinity and vice versa. The two supported each other against false claims or various misreadings of Scripture.

Much like Irenaeus, Tertullian used these polemic debates to further develop the proclamations of the Rule as well. In his work *Against Hermogenes*, Tertullian supported the affirmation of creation ex nihilo by arguing against Hermogenes's teachings that God created out of pre-existent matter. Tertullian built his case upon his interpretation of Genesis 1 and the meaning of opening phrase of Scripture, *In the beginning*.[24] This work is an example of Tertullian using the Rule of Faith as a guide not as a restriction. Tertullian was not restricted by the phrasing of the Rule, but rather was guided by the concepts passed on in the Rule. This interaction with Hermogenes also displayed Tertullian's commitment to the biblical narrative.

Along with using the Rule as a polemic device, Litfin observes that Tertullian also used the Rule as a guide for doing systematic theology.[25] In much the same manner of Irenaeus, Tertullian used the Rule to join together the Creator God of Israel proclaimed in the Hebrew Bible with Jesus and his work of salvation. The work of Christ on the cross and his resurrection must be connected and grounded upon the proclamation of God as creator. Tertullian echoed the same understanding of the principle of recapitulation as Irenaeus.

Blowers notes that the main difference between Tertullian's understanding of recapitulation and Irenaeus's work is Tertullian's emphasis on the Trinitarian dimension of the principle.[26] Tertullian noted the work of each member of the Godhead in the act of creation. This is seen clearly in his exegesis of Genesis 1:26–27,

> It was because he had already his Son close at his side, as a second Person, his own Word, and a third Person also, the Spirit in the Word, that [God] purposely adopted the plural phrase, "Let us make"; and, "in our image"; and, "become like one of us". For with whom did he create humanity? And to whom did he make humanity like? (The answer must be), the Son on the one hand, who would one day put on human nature; and the Spirit on the other, who would sanctify humanity.[27]

---

[24] See *Against Hermogenes* 20.

[25] Ibid.

[26] Blowers, *Drama of the Divine Economy*, 89.

[27] *Against Praxeas* 12.3; trans. ANF03.

Tertullian understood the special place humanity is given in this creation as bearers of the image of God. Blowers observes that Tertullian also emphasized the "utter paradox" that the magnificent restoration of all creation comes through the humble sacrifice of Jesus on the cross.[28]

Origen

In his writings, Origen stressed that there were essential, or necessary, teachings handed down from the apostles that rose above lesser teachings. In the preface of his treatise, *On First Principles*, Origen stated, "It seems on that account necessary first of all to fix a definite limit and to lay down an unmistakable rule regarding each one of these, and then to pass to the investigation of other points."[29] Origen noted a substantial list of essential teachings of the church and, much like Irenaeus and Tertullian, God as creator tops the list: "The particular points clearly delivered in the teaching of the apostles are as follow—*First*, That there is one God, who created and arranged all things, and who, when nothing existed, called all things into being—God from the first creation and foundation of the world."[30]

Like Irenaeus and Tertullian, Origen also used the Rule of Faith as a polemic device against Gnostic and Marcionite beliefs, but he used it in a slightly different way. Blowers notes that instead of using the principle of recapitulation in the manner that Irenaeus did, Origen "critically engages aspects of Platonic hierarchical cosmology to construct an ontologically 'phased' theory of creation in which the creative freedom of God and the unique revelatory and salvific role of the Logos-Christ are still secure."[31] Origen's engagement on this level has led many scholars to note that he may have held the Platonic idea of "double creation," the creation of preexistent souls and then the physical world.[32]

Peter Bouteneff notes that Origen's understanding of the doctrine of creation was also shaped by his scriptural exegesis which relied on probing the deeper meanings laid out by Scripture sometimes in an allegorical sense.[33] Bouteneff notes that Origen stressed that Genesis 1–3 should not be read literally but rather that it lays out the core narrative that God is the creator and humanity has fallen, thus leading to the redemptive work of God in Christ.[34]

---

[28] Blowers, *Drama of the Divine Economy*, 90.

[29] *On First Principles*, Preface 2; trans. *ANF04*.

[30] *On First Principles*, Preface 4. See Peter Bouteneff, *Beginnings: Ancient Christian Readings of the Biblical Creation Narratives* (Grand Rapids, MI: Baker Academic, 2008), 97 for an excellent discussion of Origen's use of the Rule.

[31] Blowers, *Drama of the Divine Economy*, 90.

[32] Ibid., 91. See also Zizioulas, *Lectures*, 86.

[33] Bouteneff, *Beginnings*, 118–19.

[34] Ibid.

The many views of Origen's interpretation of the doctrine creation show that while Origen was guided by the Rule of Faith and the primary claim of God as creator, he did not feel constricted by that single claim but rather explored the consequences of that claim in more speculative ways. For Origen, the Rule captured the core narrative of Scripture and served as a guide for theological investigation but should be seen as the starting point for further theological discourse not an end in and of itself. [35] Origen furthered the theological discourse of the doctrine of creation, taking it to uncomfortable depths of investigation for some but remaining true to the primary affirmations of Scripture.

Cappadocian Fathers

While considerable debate remains over whether the Cappadocian fathers (Basil of Caesarea, Gregory of Nazianzus, Gregory of Nyssa) have a clear doctrine of creation, Paul Blowers notes that there are certain "first principles" and theological markers that shaped the cosmology of these fathers.[36] Blowers notes that the Cappadocians balanced the Platonic views of Origen with those of Irenaeus. Like Irenaeus, they stressed God's creation of the world ex nihilo, instead of shaping the world out of preexistent matter, and God's free creative force instead of generation or emanation.[37]

Bouteneff also notes that the Cappadocian fathers used the doctrine of creation as a polemic against pagan assertions of preexistent matter and emanation.[38] They noted the importance of the teachings handed down by the apostles and contained within the core narrative of Scripture, but they also understood that further exploration and discourse were necessary.

The Cappadocians, especially Basil in *The Hexaemeron* (a collection of nine homilies on cosmology), were open to Origen's idea of double creation and further plumbed the depths of the creedal claim of God as creator.[39] Ultimately for the Cappadocian fathers, much like Irenaeus, Tertullian, and Origen before them, the doctrine of creation was a guiding

---

[35] In a discussion on the soul in *First Principles*, Origen makes a distinction between dogmatic, primary claims of theology (EIMs) and more investigative claims. He writes, "Our statement, however, that the understanding is converted into a soul, or whatever else seems to have such a meaning, the reader must carefully consider and settle for himself, as these views are not be regarded as advanced by us in a dogmatic manner, but simply as opinions, treated in the style of investigation and discussion." See *On First Principles*, 2.4.8; trans *ANF04*.

[36] Paul M. Blowers, "Beauty, Tragedy and New Creation: Theology and Contemplation in Cappadocian Cosmology," *International Journal of Systematic Theology* 18, no. 1 (2016): 7.

[37] Ibid., 15.

[38] Bouteneff, *Beginnings*, 172.

[39] See Basil, *The Hexaemeron*, Homily I.5.

factor that grounded the redemptive work of Christ and the eventual telos of humanity and all of creation.

Conclusion

It is clear from this survey that the claim of God as creator was foundational in the formation of Christian identity in the first centuries following the life of Christ. This foundational feature is underscored by its inclusion in the various renditions of the Rule of Faith and both the Nicene and Apostles' Creed. The creedal claim did not emerge in the second and third centuries but rather was drawn from the core narrative of Scripture and unfolded by the patristic theologians. We will now summarize the biblical narrative concerning the doctrine of creation that shaped and molded both the Rule of Faith and the formal creeds in order to stress that this creedal affirmation finds its origin in the narrative of Scripture and not the proclamation of a council.

Summary of the Biblical Foundation of the Doctrine

In light of the development of the doctrine of creation during the beginning centuries of Christianity, it is clear that the claim of God as creator did not emerge from the thoughts and speculations of later church fathers but rather was a foundational aspect of the Judeo-Christian narrative as seen clearly in both the Hebrew Bible and the New Testament. The theology of the church fathers and the subsequent identification of a Rule of Faith, along with the formation of formalized creeds, were guided and grounded in Scripture and the apostolic witness.

Bouteneff notes that in Irenaeus, one most clearly sees this process occurring and in many ways one sees "the Bible" taking shape, for Irenaeus used the Hebrew Bible along with the four Gospels, Paul's letters, the book of Acts, Revelation, 1 Peter and 1 and 2 John, to identify the core Christian narrative and to repudiate heretical teaching that did not match this narrative.[40] The key biblical passages that shaped this early theological and creedal development of the doctrine of creation will be summarized here.

The early church fathers recognized that Scripture clearly proclaimed God as creator with the opening lines of the book of Genesis: "In the beginning when God created the heavens and the earth" (Gen 1:1). For the Jews, this opening line clearly delineates YHWH from the pagan gods of the surrounding nations. The God of the Jews is the sole creator God and all other gods are subordinate to Him. Richard Bauckham notes that this claim

---

[40] Bouteneff, *Beginnings*, 73–74.

becomes especially pronounced in the Second Temple period, as the Jewish people cling to the preeminence of YHWH.[41]

John Walton notes that Genesis 1 provides a narratological framework for the Jewish people to understand the cause behind the beginning of the cosmos as well as to show that the world has not always been as it appears to them now.[42] Irenaeus, Tertullian, Origen, and the Cappadocian fathers used this opening line as a sharp polemic against the god fashioned by Gnostic and Marcionite thought. One also sees this opening line echoed in the New Testament (i.e., John 1:1; Acts 4:24; 14:15–17; 17:23–27), becoming a protocreedal slogan for the apostles, as already shown in the beginning of this chapter.

While Genesis 1 lays out a narrative framework, the proclamation of God as creator takes on a doxological character in the Psalms. Psalm 33:6–9 proclaims,

> By the word of the Lord the heavens were made,
>   and all their host by the breath of his mouth.
> He gathered the waters of the sea as in a bottle;
>   he put the deeps in storehouses.
> Let all the earth fear the Lord;
>   let all the inhabitants of the world stand in awe of him.
> For he spoke, and it came to be;
>   he commanded, and it stood firm.

Psalm 89:11–12a asserts,

> The heavens are yours, the earth also is yours;
>   the world and all that is in it—you have founded them.
> The north and the south—you created them;

Psalm 115:15 heralds,

> May you be blessed by the Lord,
>   who made heaven and earth.[43]

---

[41] Bauckham, "Paul's Christology," 3. Here Bauckham notes these references to God as sole creator: 2 Macc 1:24; Sir 43:33; Bel 5; Jub 12:3–5; Sib Or 3:20–35; 8:375–376; Frag 1:5–6; Frag 3; Frag 5; 2 Enoch 47:3–4; 66:4; ApAbr 7:10; Pseudo-Sophocles; JosAsen 12:1–2; TJob 2:4.

[42] John H. Walton, *Genesis*, NIV Application Commentary (Grand Rapids, MI: Zondervan, 2001), 7–8.

[43] See Ps 121:2; 124:8; and 134:3 which all use the similar phrase "made heaven and earth."

And 148:1–6 commands,

> Praise the Lord!
> Praise the Lord from the heavens;
>> praise him in the heights!
> Praise him, all his angels;
>> praise him, all his host!
> Praise him, sun and moon;
>> praise him, all you shining stars!
> Praise him, you highest heavens,
>> and you waters above the heavens!
> Let them praise the name of the Lord,
>> for he commanded and they were created.
> He established them forever and ever;
>> he fixed their bounds, which cannot be passed.

Several other psalms carry this theme as well, establishing a strong foundation for the claim of God as creator and its place among the creedal affirmations of the church.

Along with the narratological nature of Genesis 1–3 and the doxological nature of the Psalms, the prophet Isaiah used the proclamation of God as creator to ground the covenant between this God and the Hebrew people, providing hope for an exiled and persecuted people. Isaiah 42:5–8 says,

> Thus says God, the Lord,
>> who created the heavens and stretched them out,
>> who spread out the earth and what comes from it,
> who gives breath to the people upon it
>> and spirit to those who walk in it:
> I am the Lord, I have called you in righteousness,
>> I have taken you by the hand and kept you;
> I have given you as a covenant to the people,
>> a light to the nations,
>> to open the eyes that are blind,
> to bring out the prisoners from the dungeon,
>> from the prison those who sit in darkness.
> I am the Lord, that is my name;
>> my glory I give to no other,
>> nor my praise to idols.

Alister McGrath notes that the theme of God as creator is deeply imbedded in the wisdom and prophetic writings and is often connected with the theme of God as redeemer.[44] Bauckham notes that this connection is also stressed in Nehemiah and Hosea.[45]

The creator and redeemer God of Israel is also carried into the apostolic writings of the New Testament, and it is here in the New Testament that God as creator takes on clear Trinitarian implications. Paul proclaims of Christ, "He is the image of the invisible God, the firstborn of all creation; for in him all things in heaven and on earth were created, things visible and invisible, whether thrones or dominions or rulers or powers—all things have been created through him and for him. He himself is before all things, and in him all things hold together" (Col 1:15–17).

The author of Hebrews asserted, "Long ago God spoke to our ancestors in many and various ways by the prophets, but in these last days he has spoken to us by a Son, whom he appointed heir of all things, through whom he also created the worlds" (Heb 1:1–2). New Testament writers, especially Paul, also used the doctrine of creation to ground an understanding of sin and the Fall and in return the need for redemption through the work of Christ.

The creedal proclamation of God as creator, as this brief survey has shown, expresses the foundational nature of the claim and its relation to other aspects of systematic theology. The church fathers were guided by this overwhelming scriptural witness. They also explored other implications that could be drawn from it and further pursued theological inquiry without negating this fundamental assertion. Irenaeus particularly held this scriptural witness against heretical claims to show their inconsistencies with the overall core narrative of Scripture. As one saw with Origen, this essential identity marker of God as creator does not restrict further exploration and theological speculation, rather it grounds further exploration and provides a rule to assess new ideas and opinions.

Brief Survey of Seven Theological Voices (Fifth Century – Present)

From the apostolic period to Constantinople, two foundational truths are clearly asserted regarding the doctrine of creation: (1) The God of Israel and the Christian church is the sole creator God, and (2) this God created the world out of nothing. In order to note how these foundational truths have guided and grounded the discourse, this section will trace these themes in the long period of theological discourse after Constantinople up to the present. These seven theologians have been chosen for their contributions in furthering the theological discourse concerning the doctrine of creation and their understanding of the role of creedal affirmations in guiding such discourse.

---

[44] McGrath, *Christian Theology*, 296.
[45] Bauckham, "Paul's Christology," 3. See Neh 9:6 and Hos 13:4.

Augustine

The previous chapters have shown that Augustine was greatly influenced by the creedal formulations of the church. In developing his own understanding of Christian doctrine Augustine references both the Rule of Faith and the Symbol as a guide. Everett Ferguson notes that Augustine was heavily influenced by Tertullian's use of the Rule and even goes a step beyond Tertullian in connecting the Rule with the baptismal creed of his day.[46] For Augustine the Rule of Faith and the baptismal creed were guiding summaries of the core narrative of the Christian faith.

In his treatise *On Faith and the Creed*, Augustine affirmed the proclamation of God, the Father Almighty, creator of heaven and earth as fundamental in shaping Christian identity.[47] And much like Irenaeus and Tertullian before him, he used this proclamation to also affirm the principle of creation ex nihilo. Contrasting the concept of preexistent matter with the Almightiness of God, he wrote:

> For when they affirm that there is a nature which God Almighty did not create, but of which at the same time He fashioned this world, which they admit to have been disposed in beauty, they thereby deny that God is almighty, to the effect of not believing that He could have created the world without employing, for the purpose of its construction, another nature, which had been in existence previously, and which He Himself had not made.[48]

For Augustine, when the creed proclaimed God as Almighty creator it meant there is nothing above or coequal with God. Philosophies and teachings that do not affirm this do not affirm the Christian narrative described in Scripture. Simon Oliver notes that, for Augustine, creation ex nihilo is central in developing a proper doctrine of God's relation to creation.[49] In contrast to theories of emanation or construction, creation ex nihilo stresses that God is separate and greater than creation and freely sustains creation with God's own existence.

Much like the church fathers before him, Augustine used the creedal affirmations concerning creation as a guide in defending the Christian faith against various heretical leanings. God as creator separates Godself from all other lesser gods and beings. God as creator also grounds the material nature

---

[46] Everett Ferguson, *The Rule of Faith: A Guide* (Eugene, OR: Cascade Books, 2015), 30.

[47] See *On Faith and the Creed* 2.2; trans. *NPNF*1–03.

[48] Ibid.

[49] Simon Oliver, "Augustine on Creation, Providence and Motion," *International Journal of Systematic Theology* 18, no. 4 (2016): 380.

of creation. In writing against Faustus the Manichean, Augustine stressed that all aspects of creation, the physical and the spiritual, were created by God.[50]

In *Concerning the Nature of Good*, he noted, "For He is so omnipotent, that even out of nothing, that is out of what is absolutely non-existent, He is able to make good things both great and small, both celestial and terrestrial, both spiritual and corporeal."[51] Augustine also used these core creedal statements for catechetical training, especially in preparation for baptism, as noted in the previous chapter. For Augustine, God as creator was a fundamental affirmation which grounded the belief of the catechumen.

Thomas Aquinas

In Aquinas's seminal work *Summa Theologiae*, it is evident that the doctrine of creation plays a foundational role for his overarching theology. Janet Soskice notes that, more particularly, Aquinas's affirmation of creation ex nihilo serves to ground his entire doctrine of God.[52] It is of interest to note here that Aquinas followed the tradition established before him in asserting creation ex nihilo as a necessary implication of the creedal proclamation of God as creator of heaven and earth.

Soskice also notes that contemporary Aquinas scholarship, which often overplays his Aristotelianism, is beginning to stress the centrality of Scripture as foundational for his theology as well.[53] His commitment to Scripture clearly grounded his understanding of the foundational nature of the doctrine of creation. For Aquinas, the biblical narrative laid out in the book of Genesis serves as a springboard to deeper discourse on the nature of God and God's creation.

In his work *Expositio in Symbolum Apostolorum*, a commentary on the core elements of the Apostles' Creed, Aquinas observed: "It has been shown that we must first of all believe there is but one God. Now, the second is that this God is the Creator and maker of heaven and earth, of all things visible and invisible."[54] Aquinas went on to give an illustration of entering a house and feeling warmth. The further one goes into the house the warmer he gets. It is the assumption of the person, though they see no fire, that something in the house is the cause of this warmth.

---

[50] *Contra Faustum* Manichaeum, 24. 2; trans. *NPNF* 1–04.

[51] *Concerning the Nature of Good, Against the Manicheans*, 1; trans. *NPNF* 1–04.

[52] Janet Soskice, "Aquinas and Augustine on Creation and God as 'Eternal Being,'" *New Blackfriars* 95, no. 1056 (2014): 191.

[53] Ibid.

[54] Thomas Aquinas, *Expositio Symbolum Apostolorum*, Article I, paragraph 10; trans. John B. Collins, 1939, accessed at http://dhspriory.org/thomas/Creed.htm#1.

Likewise, with creation, one can assume based on the natural order and beauty of the world that there is a cause behind it. In this section, Aquinas gave three errors that are common concerning the doctrine of creation: (1) the Manichean idea that visible matter is evil; (2) the world is eternal; and (3) that God made the world using preexistent matter.[55] In briefly rebutting each of these errors, Aquinas appealed to both Scripture and the wording of the Creed.

In response to the Manichean error of considering visible matter evil and invisible matter good, he noted that it is contrary to the faith of the church and against this claim the Creed affirmed, "Of all things visible and invisible."[56] Aquinas finished this section with five benefits of the doctrine of creation. It is evident in his writings that the theological method Aquinas employed was guided by the creedal affirmations of the church, which were grounded in Scripture, but also free to explore the implications of those foundational affirmations.

Martin Luther (1483–1546)

Martin Luther's theology was deeply influenced by the creedal affirmations of the church, especially the Apostles' Creed. Luther used the Apostles' Creed as a framework for both his *Small* and *Large Catechisms*. Charles Arand notes that, for catechetical purposes, Luther rearranged the twelve articles of the faith seen in the Creed into three central articles that highlighted the Trinitarian nature of God and reflected the triadic baptismal formulas of the early church.[57]

The first article that Luther highlighted in his *Small Catechism* was the opening line of the Apostles' Creed: "I believe in God the Almighty Father, Creator of Heaven and Earth." Concerning this opening line, Luther expounded on the meaning and implications of this foundational affirmation: "I believe that God created me, along with all creatures. He gave to me: my body and soul, my eyes, ears and all the other parts of my body, my mind and all my senses. He preserves them as well."[58] Arand stresses that by opening his catechetical teaching with this article and its particular stress on God as creator, Luther understood the foundational nature of the claim and, in fact, built the rest of his theology on it.[59] For Luther, the doctrine of

---

[55] Aquinas, *Expositio Symbolum Apostolorum*, Article I, paragraph 10.

[56] Ibid.; he also cites Gen 1:1, "In the beginning God created heaven and earth" and John 1:3, "All things were made by Him."

[57] Charles P. Arand, "Luther on the Creed," *Lutheran Quarterly* 20, no. 1 (2006): 2.

[58] Martin Luther, *Small Catechism*, 2.1; trans. accessed at http://www.ccel.org/ccel/luther/smallcat.text.ii.1.html.

[59] Arand, "Luther on the Creed," 3–4.

creation signified that the world and all created beings are desperately dependent on God for existence.

Like the church fathers long before him, Luther drew out the principle of creation ex nihilo from the first article of the Apostles' Creed. Arand notes that phrase "creator of heaven and earth" utilizes the literary device *merismus*, where two extremes are used to indicate a larger more encompassing truth.[60] Creator of heaven and earth means creator of everything else in between. Luther took this idea and developed an even further truth that God is still at work creating new life out of "nothing":

> Even as God in the beginning of creation made the world out of nothing, whence He is called the Creator and the Almighty, so his manner of working continues still the same. even now and unto the end of the world, all his works are such that out of that which is nothing, worthless, despised, wretched and dead, He makes that which is something, precious, honorable, blessed and living.[61]

Luther asserted that the doctrine of creation is a statement about God and God's initial and continuing work in relation to the world. Paul Althaus notes that for Luther, "God is God because he and only he creates."[62]

John Calvin

While it has been shown that Calvin preferred to use Scripture as the foundation for his theology, Stephen Reynolds notes that his hesitancy in appealing to the ancient creeds was not doctrinal in nature but rather a desire to preserve Scripture as normative for theology.[63]

Calvin affirmed the core tenets of the creeds and understood the proclamation of God as creator to be foundational for the Christian faith, as seen in the opening of his *Institutes*. Among the several implications Calvin drew from the doctrine of creation, Cornelis Van Der Kooi highlights that Calvin aligned the doctrine of creation with the revelation of God.[64] For Calvin, God has invited creatures to know and be in relationship with Godself, as revealed through creation. In the first book of his *Institutes*, Calvin declared:

---

[60] Arand, "Luther on the Creed," 4.

[61] *The Magnificant*; trans. *The Works of Martin Luther*, Vol. III, 127.

[62] Paul Althaus, *The Theology of Martin Luther*, trans. Robert Schultz (Philadelphia, PA: Fortress Press, 1966), 105.

[63] Reynolds, "Calvin's View of the Athanasian and Nicene Creeds," 34.

[64] Cornelis Van Der Kooi, "Calvin's Theology of Creation and Providence: God's Care and Human Fragility," *International Journal of Systematic Theology* 18, no. 1 (2016): 49.

Since the perfection of blessedness consists in the knowledge of God, he has been pleased, in order that none might be excluded from the means of obtaining felicity, not only to deposit in our minds that seed of religion of which we have already spoken, but so to manifest his perfections in the whole structure of the universe, and daily place himself in our view, that we cannot open our eyes without being compelled to behold him. His essence, indeed, is incomprehensible, utterly transcending all human thought; but on each of his works his glory is engraven in characters so bright, so distinct, and so illustrious, that none, however dull and illiterate, can plead ignorance as their excuse.[65]

Calvin goes on to stress, though, that Holy Scripture is a better guide for understanding God as creator as a foundational affirmation and for also understanding God's work of redemption through Christ.[66]

Calvin's development of the doctrine of creation also displayed the effect cultural context has on the course of theological discourse. While the early church fathers developed the doctrine of creation in the context of competing Greco-Roman philosophical views, Alister McGrath notes that Calvin developed his doctrine of creation as a part of a greater world-affirming spirituality, in contrast to the world-shaming spirituality Calvin perceived from the monastic tendencies of the Catholic Church at the time. McGrath observes that Calvin perceived the world in two separate ways: as God's creation and as fallen.[67] For as much as Calvin stressed the fallen nature of creation, he ultimately viewed the world as God's creation and worthy of admiration and praise.

Karl Barth

Much like Luther, Karl Barth framed his discussion and understanding of the doctrine of creation around the opening line of the Apostles' Creed. For Barth, the confession that God is creator has as its focus the person and work of God, not the created world. In *Dogmatics in Outline,* he stressed, "It does not say, I believe in the created world, nor even, I believe in the work of creation. But, it says, I believe in God the Creator. And everything that is said about creation depends absolutely upon this Subject."[68] Barth further

---

[65] Calvin, *Institutes*, 1.5.1; trans. accessed at http://www.ccel.org/ccel/calvin/institutes.iii.vi.html.

[66] Ibid., 1.6.1.

[67] McGrath, *Christian Theology,* 299.

[68] Karl Barth, *Dogmatics in Outline*, trans. G. T. Thomson (New York: Harper & Row, 1959), 50.

stressed that natural science or so-called "creation myths" do not have as their focus and starting point God the creator but rather the created world.[69]

They begin their theories with the observed world and work their way back to an explanation. The proclamation of God as creator begins with God as the focal point and uses the claim to, in turn, explain the created world. Barth noted, "We exist and heaven and earth exist in their complete, supposed infinity, because God gives them existence. That is the great statement of the first article."[70] For Barth, the doctrine of creation does not answer the question of whether or not there is a God, but rather it poses the riddle of creation, the mysterious fact that human beings exist at all.

> How can there be something alongside God, of which he has no need? This is the riddle of creation. And the doctrine of creation answers that God, who does not need us, created heaven and earth and myself, of "sheer fatherly kindness and compassion, apart from any merit or worthiness of mine; for all of which I am bound to thank and praise Him, to serve Him and to be obedient, which is assuredly true."[71]

Citing Luther in the last half of the quoted passage above, Barth stressed that creation is an act of grace and should inspire worship and praise. Barth, though, famously disparaged the benefits of natural theology because for him Jesus is the sole source of the revelation of God. This highlights the Christocentric nature of his theology and steers worship and adoration to its proper object.

Barth also noted that the biblical creation narratives stand in direct connection with story of Israel and "God's action in covenant with man,"[72] which in turn serve as the foundation for the incarnation and the story of the redemption of this creation through the work of Jesus. Martin Henry notes that covenant and creation are interrelated for Barth, in that creation takes place for the sake of covenant.[73] For Barth, creation and covenant stand as essential elements in the Christian narrative, grounding all other doctrines.

---

[69] Barth, *Dogmatics in Outline*, 51. Barth did not consider the term myth to be proper when speaking of creation accounts because "creation as such is simply not accessible to myth." He refered to the biblical account of creation as a saga and notes that the creation accounts written of in Genesis 1 and 2 "lie outside of our historical knowledge."

[70] Ibid., 54.

[71] Ibid.

[72] Barth, *Dogmatics in Outline*, 51.

[73] Martin Henry, "Karl Barth on Creation," *Irish Theological Quarterly* 69, no. 3 (2004): 222.

Karl Rahner

As noted in the previous chapter, Karl Rahner affirmed the theology outlined by the creeds of early Christendom but asserted that they were not the final conclusions of theological discourse but rather "points of departure" for further theological investigation.[74] In terms of the doctrine of creation, Rahner affirmed the proclamation of God as creator of heaven and earth and used it as a foundational statement fundamental to understanding human beings as created beings living in a created world distinct from God.

In *Foundations of Christian Faith*, Rahner noted that humanity's "creatureliness," and therefore finitude, emphasizes that humans are both radically different from God, the infinite mystery, and also radically dependent on him.[75] Rahner used this radical difference and dependence to understand the further assertions of the church fathers' understanding of creation ex nihilo:

> Christian doctrine calls this unique relationship between God and the world the createdness of the world, its creatureliness, its ongoing being-given to itself by a personal God who establishes it freely. This establishing, then, does not have some material already at hand as its presupposition, and in this sense it is 'out of nothing.' Basically creation 'out of nothing' means to say: creation totally from God, but in such a way that the world is radically dependent on God in this creation.[76]

Rahner further insisted that this dependence of creatures on God does not make God dependent on God's creatures. Leo O'Donovan notes that for Rahner it is not that God and the world compose a larger unit that is reality, but rather that in creation God and the world are seen as radically separate.[77]

In leaving room for further theological investigation, Rahner has also stressed that the doctrine of creation and science do not have to be at odds. Rahner stressed that the church's affirmation of scientific findings should be guided, and should not contradict, the foundational affirmations of the church regarding doctrine but only so far as these affirmations of the church are regarded as certain.[78] In areas of speculation, such as the means of creation, one may explore several theories, insofar as they do not

---

[74] Migliore, *Faith Seeking Understanding*, 174. See also Rahner, "Current Problems in Christology," 149–200.

[75] Rahner, *Foundations of Christian Faith*, 77–78.

[76] Ibid., 78.

[77] Leo J. O'Donovan, *A World of Grace: An Introduction to the Themes and Foundations of Karl Rahner's Theology* (New York: Seabury Press, 1980), 46.

[78] See Karl Rahner, *Hominisation; the Evolutionary Origin of Man as a Theological Problem* (New York: Herder and Herder, 1965), section one, accessed online at http://www.religion-online.org/showchapter.asp?title=3367&C=2765.

contradict what has been revealed in Scripture, primarily that God is the creator, or in other terms, the fundamental cause of creation.

Daniel Migliore (b. 1935)

Daniel Migliore is Professor Emeritus of Theology at Princeton Theological Seminary and held the endowed title of Charles Hodge Professor of Systematic Theology during his tenure there. In his work on systematic theology, entitled *Faith Seeking Understanding*, Migliore, in the same spirit as Rahner, affirms the early Christian creeds as foundational but not constrictive. The creeds provide a framework for understanding the unique Christian identity formed in Scripture, but they were not meant as final answers regarding deeper theological discourse.

For Migliore, the spirit of the creeds should be captured and contextualized for modern readers, especially in terms of language, often stressing the need to go beyond the "surface grammar" of the creeds to what he termed its "depth grammar."[79] In stressing this, Migliore emphasized the need to understand what the creeds mean for current readers today.

In regard to the doctrine of creation, Migliore notes that it is a vitally important doctrine for today, stating, "In the first article of the Apostles' Creed, Christians affirm their faith in God the creator, 'Maker of heaven and earth.' Like all articles of the creed, this article is rich with meaning and invites inquiry. A right understanding of the confession of faith in God as creator is perhaps more important today than ever before."[80] Migliore identifies the current ecological crisis as one of the main reasons for the stressed importance of the doctrine today.

For Migliore, the doctrine of creation and the opening article of the Apostles' Creed ground a Christian's responsibility of stewardship of the created world. Migliore also notes here the current strained relationship between faith and science and follows Rahner in affirming the use of doctrine to judge modern scientific claims in light of foundational claims (i.e., God as creator).[81] If a claim of modern science does not reject the foundational claim of God as creator then one is not obliged to reject the modern claim on grounds of faith.

Implications for Teaching the Doctrine Today

As emphasized by Daniel Migliore, the doctrine of creation is a vitally important doctrine in the church's current context. The research detailed in

---

[79] Migliore, *Faith Seeking Understanding*, 75.
[80] Ibid., 96.
[81] Ibid., 117–19.

this chapter has shown that the creeds, and the protocreeds and Rules of Faith before them, have provided clear identity markers in regard to a proclamation of Christian belief concerning the doctrine. Two major affirmations have been highlighted in this chapter: (1) God as creator and (2) creation ex nihilo. While the latter is not explicitly stated in the creeds, the phrasing "heaven and earth" has been interpreted throughout the centuries proceeding the formation of the creed, and even before as seen with Irenaeus and Tertullian, as encompassing the entirety of matter, both visible and invisible.

These two identity markers have guided and shaped the theological discourse since the apostolic period, and they continue to shape the current theological conversation. Being held as essential affirmations of Scripture and Christian theology, they serve as guides in assessing contemporary claims concerning cosmic origins and development.

Rather than merely refuting these claims, the EIMs regarding the doctrine of creation enable honest dialogue across different disciplines. They provide the necessary space for dialogue because of the modest scope of the claims themselves. Samuel Powell notes that the doctrine of creation finds its authority in a regulative dimension where boundaries are drawn as to what is and what is not an essential claim of Scripture precisely because of the modesty of its claims:

> We should note, however, that what allows the regulative function to be authoritative is its modesty. Whereas in seeking to understand, the theologian is allowed to wander considerably beyond the express statements of the Christian tradition in speculative directions, the classical and regulative statements of doctrine—the creeds—impress us mainly by how much they do not say. Creeds assert that God created the world, but none goes much beyond that modest affirmation. The Christian tradition has every right to expect its adherents to embrace this affirmation, but in fact they are not being asked to commit themselves to a full-blown metaphysical system or scientific theory. To put the matter another way, the modest affirmation is compatible with many understandings.[82]

Here Powell notes the regulative nature of essential identity markers, but also the vast freedom they provide by what they do not explicitly exclude. In dialogue with the claims of modern science, further exploration and discourse is not prohibited by the creedal affirmations confessed by the church. One is not able to accept any and all claims but insofar as they do

---

[82] Samuel M. Powell, *Participating in God: Creation and Trinity* (Minneapolis, MN: Fortress Press, 2003), 8.

not contradict the essential identity markers of the Christian faith, one is open to further investigation and speculation.

In teaching the doctrine of creation today, one must begin by identifying and articulating the essential claims of the Christian faith, which are clearly supported in Scripture and have been further developed through tradition, but as Migliore stressed, one must also probe deeper and explore the open space provided by these EIMs to understand the importance of these claims for one's time.

4

Case Study 3 —
Atonement in the Creeds

This third and final case study examines the doctrine of the atonement. In many ways, the doctrine of the atonement serves as a unique case study in the larger project of understanding a creedal approach to theology. Kelly notes that while the redemptive effect of Christ's death and resurrection have always been a driving force in the development of Christian theology, "no final and universally accepted definition of the manner of its achievement has been formulated to this day."[1] L. W. Grensted, writing before Kelly, notes, "The Church, convinced of the great reality of the fact of Atonement, has never found it necessary or desirable to set her seal to any special theory for the explanation of that fact."[2] For Grensted, the creeds of early Christendom stress the reality of the fact of Christ's death and resurrection but stop short of providing a unified theory.

In this way, according to Grensted, the doctrine of the atonement is "dependent upon the Bible to a peculiar extent."[3] This dependence on Scripture also marks a dependence upon the essential identity markers drawn from Scripture. The creedal development of the doctrine of the atonement provides affirmation of the facts regarding atonement but leaves open the question of how these facts lead to the redemption of humanity. The process of developing a more thorough theory must be guided by essential identity markers in order to remain faithful to the biblical witness.

Like the previous two chapters, the structure of this chapter will consist of a survey of the early theological development of the doctrine from early creedal formulations in the biblical text through the later apostolic and patristic periods leading up to Constantinople, followed by a summary of the biblical narrative from which the EIMs are drawn and a brief survey of several key theological voices that furthered a greater understanding of the doctrine and developed more detailed theories of the atonement. The chapter will, again, conclude by briefly highlighting a few implications for teaching

---

[1] Kelly, *Early Christian Doctrine*, 163.
[2] L. W. Grensted, *A Short History of the Atonement* (Manchester, UK: Manchester University Press, 1920), 2.
[3] Ibid.

the doctrine today. As stated above, the development of the doctrine of the atonement particularly shows the benefits of using the EIM model approach to theology. In this case study, one will see the importance of establishing firm essential identity markers in order to evaluate the varying theories that have been presented over the last two millennia.

Historical Development (Apostolic Period to Constantinople)

In both the Apostles' and Nicene Creeds, one sees an affirmation of the reality of the events of Christ's death and resurrection. They affirm the suffering of Christ under Pontius Pilate, his crucifixion, death, burial, and resurrection. They also affirm the remission of sins, with the Constantinopolitan version of the Nicene Creed aligning this remission with the act of baptism. Yet as noted above, they do not connect the two ideas in any formal way. This is not an oversight of these formulations but rather a reflection of the historical development of the doctrine.

In his early sermons recorded in the book of Acts, Peter similarly focused on the events of Christ's death and resurrection, aligning them with the fulfillment of prophecy but stopping short of providing a deeper understanding of their effect on the forgiveness of sins.[4] Paul, however, provided a direct connection between the death of Jesus and the forgiveness of sins. In referencing an early Christian creedal formulation, Paul affirmed in 1 Cor 15:3–4:

> For I handed on to you as of first importance what I in turn had received:
> that Christ died for our sins in accordance with the scriptures,
> and that he was buried,
> and that he was raised on the third day in accordance with the scriptures.

By attributing this statement of belief to an earlier tradition, Paul reflected the belief of the greater church not only his own. Neufeld stresses that the *paradosis* language used by Paul highlights the primitive nature of the claim.[5] In this early creedal proclamation one sees a direct connection, perhaps the first, between the death of Christ and the forgiveness of sins. Kelly notes that this passage was most likely compiled to summarize the core narrative of the Christian message.[6] This, then, marks Christ's death for

---

[4] See Acts 2:14–36; 3:11–26; 10:34–43. In 10:34–43 as Peter is speaking to Cornelius' family, he does stress though, "All the prophets testify about him that everyone who believes in him receives forgiveness of sins through his name" (v. 43).

[5] Neufeld, *Earliest Christian Confessions*, 47.

[6] Kelly, *Early Christian Creeds*, 17.

the sins of humanity as an essential identity marker in the development of Christian doctrine.

The first epistle of Peter makes a similar connection between Christ's death and humanity's sin by alluding to the Suffering Servant passage from the prophet Isaiah:

> For to this you have been called, because Christ also suffered for you, leaving you an example, so that you should follow in his steps. "He committed no sin, and no deceit was found in his mouth." When he was abused, he did not return abuse; when he suffered, he did not threaten; but he entrusted himself to the one who judges justly. He himself bore our sins in his body on the cross, so that, free from sins, we might live for righteousness; by his wounds you have been healed. For you were going astray like sheep, but now you have returned to the shepherd and guardian of your souls. (1 Pet 2:21–25; c.f. Isa 53)

With this connection, Peter aligned the suffering of Jesus with the sin and redemption of humanity. Christ's suffering and death provides a way for the salvation and righteousness.

The connection between the death of Christ and the forgiveness of sin is further developed in the various renditions of the Rule of Faith that were formulated during the apostolic and early patristic periods. Among the nine "unchanging, absolute truths" that Litfin draws from the various renditions of the Rule, he notes that "the act of crucifixion for the purpose of salvation" serves as a linchpin.[7] For Litfin, the Rule of Faith captures the core narrative of the Christian message, which guided the theological development of early Christian theology. Disregard for any of the nine truths would be a step away from Christian theology. An examination of the early theological development of the concept of atonement will best show how the tradition passed down by the apostles was carried on in the first three centuries of the church.

Throughout various writings, the earliest of the apostolic fathers carried on the tradition passed down to them and carefully connected the reality of Christ's sacrifice with the redemption of humanity. Clement of Rome (AD 30–100) in his first letter to the Corinthians extoled them to "look steadfastly to the blood of Christ, and see how precious that blood is to God, which, having been shed for our salvation, has set the grace of repentance before the whole world."[8] Ignatius of Antioch (AD 30–107)

---

[7] Litfin, "Learning," under "2477."

[8] *1 Clement* 7; trans. *ANF* 01. See also *1 Clement* 21: "Let us reverence the Lord Jesus Christ, whose blood was given for us" and 49: "On account of the Love he bore us, Jesus Christ our Lord gave His blood for us by the will of God; His flesh for our flesh, and His soul for our souls."

affirmed in his rendition of the Rule of Faith that Christ was "truly, under Pontius Pilate and Herod the tetrarch, nailed [to the cross] for us in His flesh."[9] He also claimed "our Savior Jesus Christ, which suffered for our sins"[10] and "according to Jesus Christ, who died for us, in order, by believing in His death, ye may escape from death."[11]

In his letter to the Philippians, Polycarp (AD 65–100) explicitly quoted from 1 Pet 2:24 affirming that Christ bore or sins on the cross.[12] He also connected Christ's death and resurrection with redemption: "Him who died for us, and for our sakes was raised again by God from the dead."[13] In these early proclamations of the apostolic fathers one sees a connection between the death of Christ and the atonement for one's sins, but they do not develop further a unified theory as to why or how Christ's death atoned for sins. Grensted notes, "It was not in theory but in life that the Living Fact approved itself to men, and so it is natural that the earliest days of the Church should be marked by emphasis upon the atonement as a fact. Of theory there is none."[14]

Irenaeus

With Irenaeus, one sees a more comprehensive understanding of God's strategy for redemption beginning to develop. In his rendition of the Rule of Faith, Irenaeus focused on the established events of Christ's life: his incarnation and virgin birth, suffering under Pontius Pilate, his death, resurrection, and ascension.[15] Based on these events, Irenaeus recognized Jesus as "the Savior of those who are saved."[16]

In a shorter summary of his Rule in the opening of *Against Heresies*, he affirmed belief in "one Christ Jesus, the Son of God, incarnate for our salvation."[17] For Irenaeus, the incarnation, death, and resurrection of Jesus prepare a way for the redemption of humanity. His Rule, then, recognizes that the events of Jesus's life were a part of the greater strategy put in place by God for the redemption of the world.

Irenaeus framed his understanding of atonement through the principle of recapitulation, as noted in the previous chapter. In brief, for Irenaeus recapitulation understands the redemption of humanity as part of

---

[9] *Epistle to the Smyrneans* 1; trans. *ANF* 01.
[10] Ibid., 7.
[11] *Epistle to the Trallians* 2; trans. *ANF* 01.
[12] *Epistle to the Philippians* 8.
[13] Ibid., 9; trans. *ANF* 01.
[14] Grensted, *A Short History*, 11.
[15] *Against Heresies* 3.4.2 (See also 1.10.1).
[16] Ibid.
[17] Ibid., 1.10.1; trans. Greenslade, *Early Latin Theology*, 65.

the complete story of God's interaction with humanity beginning with creation. The rescue effort completed by the death and resurrection of Jesus was not a secondary plan put together after the Fall, but rather a seamless part of the divine strategy. Blowers notes that recapitulation cannot be "reduced to cosmology, Christology, or soteriology because it integrates them all."[18] For Irenaeus, creation and redemption are interconnected themes and cannot be separated; hence a more complete principle like that of recapitulation captures the complexity of the divine strategy.

Eric Osborn notes that at least eleven themes can be drawn from Irenaeus's understanding of recapitulation: "unification, repetition, redemption, perfection, inauguration and consummation, totality, the triumph of Christus Victor, ontology, epistemology and ethics."[19] Osborn also notes that the divine action of recapitulation ultimately accomplishes four things: it (1) corrects and then (2) perfects humanity as well as (3) inaugurating and (4) consummating a new humanity.[20]

For Irenaeus, the incarnation plays just as a significant role in the act of recapitulation, and ultimately the act of redemption, as the cross. The Fall made it necessary that Christ would take on flesh and unite fallen humanity with the divine nature in order to restore humanity to its original nature. Irenaeus, following the Apostle Paul, noted that in the incarnation Jesus becomes the New Adam. Gustaf Wingren notes that, for Irenaeus, "if man is to be saved, it is necessary that the first man, Adam, be brought back to life, and not simply that a new and perfect man who bears no relation to Adam should appear on earth."[21]

Wingren also notes that for Irenaeus this means that in order to redeem humanity Jesus had to experience authentic humanity: thirst, hunger, sorrow, joy, and death.[22] Irenaeus then stressed that Christ as the New Adam unites all of humanity with him in his death on the cross. Appealing extensively to the writings of both Paul and Peter, he observed, "Jesus Christ, the Son of God, is one and the same, who did by suffering reconcile us to God, and rose from the dead; who is at the right hand of the Father, and perfect in all things."[23] Irenaeus also viewed the incarnation, death, and resurrection of Jesus as declaring God's victory over the enemy who led the first Adam into captivity: "He [Jesus] has therefore, in His work of recapitulation, summed up all things, both waging war against our enemy,

---

[18] Blowers, *Drama*, 87.

[19] Eric Francis Osborn, *Irenaeus of Lyons* (Cambridge, UK: Cambridge University Press, 2001), 97–98.

[20] Ibid., 97.

[21] Gustaf Wingren, *Man and the Incarnation: A Study in the Biblical Theology of Irenaeus* (Philadelphia, PA: Muhlenberg Press, 1959), 95.

[22] Ibid.

[23] *Against Heresies* 3.16.9; trans. *ANF* 01.

and crushing him who had at the beginning led us away captives in Adam."[24]

  With Irenaeus and the principle of recapitulation one sees a more developed understanding of the overall story of God, yet Irenaeus remained relatively focused on the actions of Jesus: creation, incarnation, suffering, death, resurrection and ascension. As captured in his Rule of Faith, the essential elements of God's work in redemption center on the person and work of Jesus. Much like the apostolic fathers before him, though, he explicitly developed little in the way of an overall theory of atonement.[25]

Tertullian

With Tertullian, one sees a similar approach as Irenaeus. Tertullian, in his rendition of the Rule of Faith, stressed the factual events of Jesus's life and work: the incarnation via the virgin birth, his preaching and miracles, his crucifixion and resurrection.[26] It is interesting to note that neither Irenaeus nor Tertullian felt it necessary to develop a strong philosophical/theological understanding of why the death and resurrection of Christ redeemed humanity and atoned for their sin. The essential identity markers of Christian theology were, for them, related to the person and work of Christ in relation to God the Father and the Holy Spirit.

  In writing against the heresy of Marcion, though, Tertullian did stress the importance of the cross and Christ's death in terms of the entire Christian message:

> Christ's death, wherein lies the whole weight and fruit of the Christian name, is denied although the apostle asserts it so expressly as undoubtedly real, making it the very foundation of the gospel, of our salvation and of his own preaching. "I have delivered unto you before all things," says he, "how that Christ died for our sins, and that he was buried, and that He rose again the third day."[27]

Here Tertullian noted the tradition passed down from Paul and stressed that one must affirm the reality of Christ's humanity and actual death in order to align with that tradition. He also noted that this death was prophetically grounded in the Hebrew Bible. Referencing the golden serpent from the book of Exodus, he wrote:

---

   [24] *Against Heresies* 5.21.1; trans. *ANF* 01.

   [25] Osborn, appealing to Aulen, does note hints of Christus Victor, but as a theory it is not explicitly developed by Irenaeus.

   [26] See *Prescriptions Against Heretics*, 13.

   [27] *Against Marcion* 3.8; trans. *ANF* 03.

Did he not here also intend to show the power of our Lord's cross, whereby that old serpent the devil was vanquished,—whereby also to every man who was bitten by spiritual serpents, but who yet turned with an eye of faith to it, was proclaimed a cure from the bite of sin, and health for evermore?[28]

Here is both a reference to victory over Satan as well as a personal cure for sin. One also notes that, for Tertullian, the death of Christ was a central message of both the Hebrew Bible and the New Testament.

Tertullian also carried on the principle of recapitulation developed by Irenaeus. For Tertullian, redemption and creation are connected as parts of the divine strategy in dealing with fallen humanity. The cross is the ultimate reversal of the reversal set in motion by Adam. Blowers notes that Tertullian emphasized "the utter paradox, the sheer unlikelihood, the seemingly absurd fact that the final and complete correction of the cosmic disaster of the primal fall comes through the weakness of incarnation and the folly of the cross."[29] The complete work of recapitulation redeems humanity and displays God as the supreme savior. Tertullian used this principle to run counter to the Gnostic and Marcion heresies he faced.

While Tertullian did not offer a more developed theory of the atonement, he did emphasize the salvific benefits of the cross. Quoting from the first epistle of John, he affirmed that "the blood of His Son purifieth us utterly from every sin" and that Jesus is the "propitiation for our sins."[30] He also noted that the goats on the Day of Atonement can be understood as representing types of Christ. These remarks have led some to propose that Tertullian planted the seed of the substitution theory.[31] Kelly notes that while these remarks "may well contain the germ of a doctrine of substitution," Tertullian did not develop them in a deeper way.[32] For Tertullian, Christ's death is fundamentally connected to the redemption of humanity as affirmed in Scripture.

---

[28] *Against Marcion* 3.18; trans. *ANF* 03.

[29] Blowers, *Drama*, 89–90; See also *Against Marcion* 2.2.4; 5.5.9.

[30] *On Modesty* 19; trans. *ANF* 04; cf. 1 John 1:7; 2:2.

[31] See Peter Ensor, "Tertullian and Penal Substitutionary Atonement," *Evangelical Quarterly* 82, no. 2 (2014): 130–42, for a comprehensive discussion.

[32] Kelly, *Early Christian Doctrines*, 177. It could also be noted that Tertullian's concept of "satisfaction" leans more toward human agency in regard to salvation. See Grensted, *A Short History*, 30.

Origen

As noted in previous chapters, Origen's theology, much like Irenaeus's and Tertullian's, was guided and shaped by essential identity markers. Origen's Rule of Faith affirms the fundamental facts about the God of Christianity in his Triune nature. After affirming God as creator of heaven and earth, Origen affirmed the central points of the person and work of Jesus Christ:

> *Secondly*, That Jesus Christ Himself, who came (into the world), was born of the Father before all creatures; that, after He had been the servant of the Father in the creation of all things—"For by Him were all things made"—He in the last times, divesting Himself (of His glory), became a man, and was incarnate although God, and while made a man remained the God which He was; that He assumed a body like to our own, differing in this respect only, that it was born of a virgin and of the Holy Spirit: that this Jesus Christ was truly born, and did truly suffer, and did not endure this death common (to man) in appearance only, but did truly die; that He did truly rise from the dead; and that after His resurrection He conversed with His disciples, and was taken up (into heaven).[33]

Here Origen, like the Fathers before him, emphasized the reality of the events of Christ's incarnation, death, and resurrection. The atonement is a result of the Christ event. Grensted stresses that during the first two centuries after the apostles, "redemption remained throughout a fact rather than a doctrine."[34] Origen did, though, springboard from this fact to speculate on the inner workings of the atonement.

While Irenaeus and Tertullian worked from frameworks of recapitulation, Origen developed further the concept of ransom in regard to atonement. The notion that Christ's death pays the debt incurred by the sin had been developed prior, but Origen took the idea further and began to fill in the details of the idea. If Christ's death is a payment for sin, then to whom was the payment directed? For Origen, the only plausible answer could be Satan.

In his commentary on the Gospel of Matthew, Origen wrote, "To whom was it paid? Certainly not God; can it then be to the evil one? for he had the power over us until the ransom given to him on our behalf, namely the life of Jesus; and he was deceived thinking that he could keep his soul in

---

[33] *On First Principles*, Preface 4; trans. *ANF* 04.
[34] Grensted, *A Short History*, 33. Grensted goes on to note that the fact of Redemption, though, was used to test other doctrines like the Trinity and the Incarnation.

his power."[35] He further developed this thought in his commentary on the book of Romans. In reference to the Pauline idea of "bought with a price"[36] he wrote:

> Now it was the devil that held us, to whose side we had been drawn away by our sins. He asked, therefore, as our price the blood of Christ. But until the blood of Jesus, which was so precious that alone it sufficed for the redemption of all, was given, it was necessary that those who were established in the Law should give each for himself his blood (i.e. in circumcision) as it were in imitation of the redemption that was to be.[37]

Grensted notes that the idea that God paying a ransom to Satan lessens the ultimate power of God did not appear to occur to Origen.[38] This ransom did not contradict the essential identity markers detailed in his Rule of Faith. It went beyond them, for sure, but did not negate them therefore it was a path worth exploring.

Kelly notes that Origen also opened the door to viewing the death of Christ as a substitutionary sacrifice.[39] Origen professed that Christ took on the sins of humanity and as its high priest he offered a propitiatory sacrifice.[40] He not only offered the sacrifice, but Christ himself was the spotless lamb required for atonement.[41] Origen, like Irenaeus and Tertullian before him, also appealed to Isaiah 53 in understanding Christ as the suffering servant, suffering on behalf of the sins of the world: "He too has borne our sins and has been bruised because of our iniquities, and the punishment which was owing to us, in order that we might be chastised and might obtain peace, has fallen on Him."[42]

Kelly notes that while the two ideas, ransom and substitution, seem irreconcilable, for Origen they both fit into a greater scheme of understanding the ultimate restoration of the entirety creation, both visible and invisible.[43] It should be stressed here, again, that Origen did not fully develop either concepts into a systematic doctrine, but rather noted each as an element of a larger complex truth.

---

[35] *In Matthew* 16.8; trans. Henry Bettenson, ed., *The Early Christian Fathers* (Oxford, UK: Oxford University Press, 1956), 224.

[36] 1 Cor 6:20; 7:23.

[37] *In Romans* 2.13; trans. Grensted, *A Short History*, 37.

[38] Grensted, *A Short History*, 38.

[39] Kelly, *Early Christian Doctrines*, 186.

[40] *In Romans* 3.8.

[41] *Homilies in Numbers* 24.1.

[42] *In Ioh* 28; trans. Kelly, *Early Christian Doctrines*, 186.

[43] Kelly, *Early Christian Doctrines*, 186.

Cappadocian Fathers

In the fourth century, the Cappadocian father Gregory of Nyssa further developed the ransom to Satan idea. Baker and Green note that, for Gregory, the justice of God would not allow atonement for sin without proper payment.[44] For Gregory, much like Origen, the debt of humanity's sin was not owed to God but rather Satan, who owned humanity as slaves. Christ, a prize of far greater value, was offered to Satan in exchange for humanity. Gregory's understanding of the ransom theory relies on a bit of deception on the part of God. Satan accepts the exchange, not knowing that he will be unable to possess Christ in the same way that he did humanity.

Christ's glory is hidden in the taking on of flesh. Gregory stressed: "In order to secure that the ransom on our behalf might be easily accepted by him who required it, the Deity was hidden under the veil of our nature, that so, as with ravenous fish, the hook of the Deity might be gulped down along with the bait of flesh."[45] Through this deception God displayed his justice and mercy in providing ransom for humanity. While lacking explicit biblical support, Grensted notes that Gregory's theory remained a prominent theory of the Atonement up until the time of Anselm.[46]

A main critic of Gregory's view, though, was his fellow Cappadocian Father Gregory of Nazianzus. Gregory of Nazianzus thoroughly rejected the idea that Christ was offered to Satan as payment of ransom, and he also denied that the payment was made to God.

> Now, since a ransom belongs only to him who holds in bondage, I ask to whom was this offered, and for what cause? If to the Evil One, fie upon the outrage! If the robber receives ransom, not only from God, but a ransom which consists of God Himself, and has such an illustrious payment for his tyranny, a payment for whose sake it would have been right for him to have left us alone altogether. But if to the Father, I ask first, how? For it was not by Him that we were being oppressed; and next, On what principle did the Blood of His Only begotten Son delight the Father, Who would not receive even Isaac, when he was being offered by his Father, but changed the sacrifice, putting a ram in the place of the human victim?[47]

---

[44] Mark D. Baker and Joel B. Green, *Recovering the Scandal of the Cross: Atonement in New Testament & Contemporary Contexts* (Downers Grove, IL: InterVarsity Press, 2000), 147. See also Gregory of Nyssa, *Greater Catechism* 22–23. Gregory notes there, "His making the redemption of the captive a matter of exchange exhibits His justice." English trans. Grensted, *A Short History*, 39.

[45] *Greater Catechism* 24; trans. Grensted, *A Short History*, 40.

[46] Grensted, *A Short History*, 41.

[47] Gregory of Nazianzus, *Oration* 45, 22; trans. access at http://www.newadvent.org/fathers/310245.htm.

Gregory of Nazianzus instead viewed the purpose and the power of the cross through the lens of sacrifice. It is through sacrifice that death is defeated and the cure for sin is unveiled. Here Gregory of Nazianzus noted the golden serpent of Num 21:9.[48]

The differing views of Gregory of Nyssa and Gregory of Nazianzus highlight the complex nature of theological investigation regarding the doctrine of the Atonement. Both fathers affirmed the factual elements of Christ's incarnation, death, and resurrection. Their disagreement shows the freedom provided in theological discourse to explore the deeper details of the doctrine. Differing theories may be presented and tested against Scripture and reason.

Conclusion

Kelly captures the complexity of surveying the patristic understanding of the doctrine of the atonement when he notes that with the church fathers one finds "a variety of theories, to all appearance unrelated and even mutually incompatible, existing side by side and sometimes sponsored by the same theologian."[49] Three prominent ideas have been identified: recapitulation, ransom, and sacrifice. Each displays an understanding of the essential identity markers regarding the atonement and a desire to understand the deeper details that lie within that uniquely Christian identity.

As stressed above, no one unified theory was presented and developed during this time. Vincent Brümmer notes that the theories of the early fathers should be viewed as "alternative metaphors that the Fathers use to indicate the meaning of the atonement without any attempt to develop them systematically or to integrate them in a coherent whole."[50] The various theories were not mere theological inventions but rather varying interpretations of the complex biblical narrative.

Summary of the Biblical Foundation of the Doctrine

The complex nature of the patristic understanding of the atonement is due in large part to the multifarious nature of the biblical narrative. With the biblical narrative one will note several expressions of the purpose and benefit of the death and resurrection of Christ. It is the purpose of this section to highlight key references within the biblical narrative that give

---

[48] Nazianzus, *Oration* 45, 22.

[49] Kelly, *Early Christian Doctrine*, 375.

[50] Vincent Brümmer, *Atonement, Christology and the Trinity: Making Sense of Christian Doctrine* (Aldershot, England: Ashgate, 2005), 69.

shape to these different expressions, which in order gave shape to the theological discourse of the first three centuries and beyond.

Among the various expressions of the purpose and benefit of the death and resurrection of Christ, one will specifically note references to Christ's death being for humanity, in terms of ransom, substitution, and sacrificial language, as well as his death and resurrection representing the ultimate triumph or victory over death and evil. The centrality of the cross should also be noted within the biblical narrative. It is given considerable examination in each of the four Gospels, with Mark devoting close to half of his Gospel to it. Donald Macleod notes that given this proportional emphasis, the Gospel writers were keenly aware that the death and resurrection of Jesus were central to understanding Jesus's overall mission.[51]

The first affirmation of the biblical narrative is that Christ's death and resurrection were on *behalf of* humanity, or *for* humanity. As noted in the previous section, Paul, carrying on an earlier protocreedal tradition, affirmed that a central element of the story of Jesus is that he died for humanity's sins (1 Cor 15:3). The Nicene Creed captures this idea when, before listing the facts of the incarnation, cross, and resurrection, it simply states, "who for us men, and for our salvation." In presenting this central point, though, the biblical narrative uses a variety of linguistic devices. It speaks of the purpose and function of the cross in terms of ransom, substitution, and sacrifice.

In terms of ransom, Jesus himself stated, "For the Son of Man came not to be served but to serve, and to give his life a ransom for many" (Mark 10:45).[52] The protocreedal statement captured in 1 Timothy states, "For there is one God; there is also one mediator between God and humankind, Christ Jesus, himself human, who gave himself a ransom for all" (1 Tim 2:5–6). Peter also stressed, "You know that you were ransomed from the futile ways inherited from your ancestors, not with perishable things like silver or gold, but with the precious blood of Christ, like that of a lamb without defect or blemish" (1 Peter 1:18–19). In the book of Revelation, the new song sung to Christ emphasizes, "by your blood you ransomed for God saints from every tribe and language and people and nation" (Rev 5:9).

In terms of substitution, Jesus is often presented as suffering on the cross *on humanity's behalf.* Paul stressed this most clearly in his writing. In his letter to the Galatian church, he noted, "Christ redeemed us from the curse of the law by becoming a curse for us" (Gal 3:13). In 1 Cor 5:15, he stated, "And he died for all, so that those who live might live no longer for themselves." He also stressed Christ as one "who loved me and gave himself for me" (Gal 2:20; cf. Eph 5:2). In the passage referenced in the previous

---

[51] Donald Macleod, *Christ Crucified: Understanding the Atonement* (Downers Grove, IL: InterVarsity Press, 2014), 16.

[52] See Matt 20:28.

section, Peter also depicted Christ's death as a substitute for humanity's punishment (1 Pet 2:21). In this passage Peter referenced the Suffering Servant in Isaiah who "was wounded for our transgressions, crushed for our iniquities; upon him was the punishment that made us whole, and by his bruises we are healed" (Isa 53:5).

The substitutionary language used to depict Christ's death also appeals to the concept of sacrifice. Paul noted that "Christ loved us and gave himself up for us, a fragrant offering and sacrifice to God" (Eph 5:2) and that "God put [Jesus] forward as a sacrifice of atonement by his blood, effective through faith" (Rom 3:25a). The writer of Hebrews clearly aligned Christ with the Jewish sacrificial system. "He entered once for all into the Holy Place, not with the blood of goats and calves, but with his own blood, thus obtaining eternal redemption" (Heb 9:12).

The biblical narrative also used the language of victory to express the significance of Christ's death and resurrection, a point well observed by the early church. The writer of Hebrews, while clearly depicting Jesus as the sacrificial lamb, also noted, "Since, therefore, the children share flesh and blood, he himself likewise shared the same things, so that through death he might destroy the one who has the power of death, that is, the devil" (Heb 2:14). 1 John 3:8b proclaims, "The Son of God was revealed for this purpose, to destroy the works of the devil." Paul stressed that Jesus triumphantly rescues us from "this present evil age" (Gal 1:4), enslavement to "the elemental spirits of the world" (Gal 4:3), and "the power of darkness" (Col 1:12).

By refraining from developing a formal proclamation of a unified and comprehensive theory of the atonement, the early church fathers recognized the many expressions of the significance of the death and resurrection of Christ detailed in the biblical narrative. The creedal development of the doctrine was driven by the facts of the Christ event and allowed each of these expressions found in the biblical narrative the proper space to be developed further.

Brief Survey of Seven Theological Voices (Fifth Century – Present)

While no formal, unified theory of the atonement emerged within the first three centuries of the church, several themes drawn from the biblical narrative guided and shaped the theological discourse of the time. This section will turn to seven key theological voices that further explored the purpose and meaning of these themes in order to construct a more comprehensive understanding of the doctrine of the atonement.

Particular attention will be shown as to how the essential identity markers articulated by the creeds and the various themes presented in the biblical narrative shaped this further exploration. These seven voices have been chosen for their contributions in furthering the theological discourse concerning the doctrine of the atonement and their understanding of the role of creedal affirmations in guiding such discourse.

Augustine

The previous two case studies have sufficiently displayed the role and influence of the Rule of Faith and the creeds in shaping Augustine's theology. In terms of the atonement, he affirms the great facts of the Christ event. In *On Faith and the Creed*, he proclaimed, "Therefore do we believe in Him Who Under Pontius Pilate Was Crucified And Buried."[53] For Augustine, Christ was humiliated "on our behalf"[54] in both his incarnation and death, appealing to Phil 2:8. He also viewed the burial as a key element referenced in the Creed for it depicts new life being formed in that same way Christ's human life was formed in Mary's womb. Augustine affirmed that the resurrection was also for us, that Christ is "the first-begotten for brethren to come after Him."[55]

Augustine also began to further explore the themes drawn out by the fathers before him. Grensted notes that Augustine, building upon the teaching of Ambrose, stressed the theme of the justice of God, which "appealed strongly to the legal mind of the West."[56] In his treatise *On the Trinity*, Augustine observed, "The death of the sinner springing from the necessity of condemnation is deservedly abolished by the death of the Righteous One springing from the freed choice of His compassion."[57] By highlighting the theme of justice, Augustine downplayed the role of Satan in the transaction. Grensted notes that by shifting the focus to the just nature of the Godhead Augustine prepared the way for the God-focused theories of Anselm and those after.[58]

Augustine also explored the themes of substitution and sacrifice. Christ's suffering and death under Pontius Pilate, as attested by the creed, became the ultimate sacrifice on behalf of humanity. In *On the Holy Trinity*, he further wrote:

> The bonds of many sins in many deaths were loosed, through the one death of the One which no sin had preceded. Which death, though not due, the Lord therefore rendered for us, that the death which was due might work us no hurt . . . Whereas by His death the one most real

---

[53] *On Faith and the Creed* 5.11; trans. *NPNF1–03*.
[54] Ibid.
[55] Ibid., 5.12.
[56] Grensted, *A Short History*, 89–90.
[57] *On the Holy Trinity* 4.2.4; trans. *NPFP1–03*.
[58] Grensted, *A Short History*, 91.

sacrifice was offered up for us, whatever fault there was whence principalities and powers held us fast as of right to pay its penalty, He cleansed, abolished, extinguished.[59]

McGrath notes that for Augustine, Christ is both the sacrificial lamb and the priest.[60] Augustine's understanding of the cross as an atoning sacrifice prepares the way for Anselm's famous work as well.

Anselm (1033–1109)

Theological discourse after Augustine highlighted the various themes articulated by the early church fathers but still left the doctrine of the atonement underdeveloped until the time of Anselm. Anselm, who himself was heavily influenced by Augustine, sought to explore beyond the established facts and inferred themes of Christ's incarnation, death, and resurrection. Anselm affirmed the facts of the Christ event as established by the conciliar creeds of the church and the various themes highlighted by the church fathers, but he used them to guide further theological exploration and development.

William Mann notes that all of Anselm's theology was guided "necessarily by authority, the authority of Scripture (the revealed word of God), the authority of confessional creeds formulated by Church councils (in particular, the Nicene Creed), and the authority of the church fathers (in particular, Augustine)."[61] In terms of the authority of conciliar creeds, Anselm did not consider them exhaustive lists of final answers on the sum of theology. They were essential markers that provided the freedom for further discussion.

In *On the Procession of the Holy Spirit*, he noted, "For we know that the creed has not expressed everything that we ought to believe and profess, nor did those who prescribed the creed wish that the Christian faith be content to believe and profess the things that the creed posited."[62] Anselm also noted that new theological developments are not corruptions of creedal theology so long as they "add nothing contrary to the things said in the creed."[63]

---

[59] *On the Holy Trinity* 4.13.17.

[60] McGrath, *Christian Theology*, 412; See also *City of God* 10.

[61] William E. Mann, "Anselm on the Trinity," in *The Cambridge Companion to Anselm*, ed. by Brian Davies and Brian Leftow (Cambridge, UK: Cambridge University Press, 2004), 258.

[62] *On the Procession of the Holy Spirit* 13; trans. *Anselm of Canterbury: The Major Works* (Oxford, UK: Oxford University Press, 1998), 426. In this work, the creed Anselm is referencing is the Nicene Creed.

[63] Ibid.

In his landmark work *Cur Deus Homo*, Anselm developed the first formal doctrine of the atonement. As noted in the title of the work, Anselm sought to explain the necessity of the incarnation and crucifixion in dealing with humanity's sin. Berard Marthaler notes that by building on the feudal system prevalent in his time Anselm developed a doctrine of the atonement that appealed to the satisfaction of the debt incurred to God by the sin of humanity.[64] The offense of sin was so great that God could not simply forgive humanity. Human beings, because of their sin and finiteness, were not able to satisfy the debt; therefore God had to become a human being and die a sacrificial death in order to atone for the sins of humanity.

For Anselm, the incarnation and crucifixion are vitally connected. Since a human being incurred the debt, a human being must make the satisfaction. Since God is the one slighted, though, no one other than God could truly make amends. Out of love for humanity Jesus takes on human flesh and satisfies the punishment for sin, though he was without sin. As will be noted below, Anselm's theory of satisfaction greatly influenced the theological landscape of the Reformation and still provides a theological and philosophical foundation for substitutionary atonement theories.

Thomas Aquinas

As noted in the previous chapter, Aquinas affirmed the articles of the Apostles' Creed in his commentary on the creed, *Expositio in Symbolum Apostolorum*. In affirming that Christ suffered crucifixion, death, and burial under Pontius Pilate, Aquinas went further to answer why Christ had to suffer in this way. He listed two reasons: (1) the cross was a remedy against sin as well as (2) an example of how one should sacrificially live.[65]

For Aquinas, the cross as a remedy for sin cures five evils incurred by sin. The second evil incurred is that sin commits an offense against God. With this second evil incurred by sin, Aquinas followed Anselm's theme of satisfaction. The offense must be amended but human beings, weakened by sin, are incapable of making proper satisfaction, and therefore Christ had to enter the world and take on humanity.

Grensted notes that for Aquinas, much like Augustine and Anselm, the incarnation was essentially linked with the atonement.[66] He also notes, though, that Aquinas does not go as far as Anselm in proclaiming their necessity.[67] In his *Summa*, Aquinas nuanced the word *necessity* to show that

---

[64] Berard L. Marthaler, *The Creed: The Apostolic Faith in Contemporary Theology* (Mystic, CT: Twenty-Third Publications, 1987), 157.

[65] *Expositio Symbolum Apostolorum*, Article 4, paragraph 3.

[66] Grensted, *A Short History*, 150.

[67] Ibid., 151.

it is both unnecessary and necessary.[68] It is unnecessary in this sense that no outside force or rule compelled God to act. It was necessary, however, to achieve the end goal of humanity's redemption. Eleonore Stump notes that, for Aquinas, in one sense God could have "willed to free humans from sin without any satisfaction" without acting against justice, and yet in another sense there was no better way to redeem humanity than to make satisfaction.[69]

Stump also notes that among a number of subsidiary roles Aquinas assigned making satisfaction as a general role to the passion and death of Christ.[70] In regard to making satisfaction, Aquinas followed Anselm's lead. In his *Compendium Theologica*, Aquinas asserted, "To save us, consequently, Christ was not content merely to make our possibility His portion, but he willed actually to suffer that He might satisfy for our sins. He endured for us those sufferings which we deserved to suffer in consequence of the sin of our first parent."[71] Aquinas went on to note, though, that Christ death did more than satisfy a debt. It also exemplified a life of virtue, obedience, and fortitude.[72]

Martin Luther

In both Luther's *Large* and *Small Catechisms*, he proclaimed and affirmed the articles of the Apostles' Creed. In regard to the second article, Luther stressed that the incarnation, death, and resurrection of Jesus sum up the story of redemption found in the biblical narrative and serve to ground the entire Gospel. In his writings Luther highlighted and further developed the theme of satisfaction. In his *Large Catechism*, he stressed that Jesus "suffered, died and was buried, that He might make satisfaction for me and pay what I owe, not with silver nor gold, but with His precious blood."[73]

Matthieu Arnold notes that Luther presented himself as the "heir of the Western Christian tradition," which viewed Christ as the God-man who appeased the wrath of God against sin through his sacrificial and

---

[68] *Summa Theologica* 3 Q47.

[69] Eleonore Stump, "Atonement According to Aquinas," in *Oxford Readings in Philosophical Theology. Volume 1, Trinity, Incarnation, and Atonement*, ed. by Michael C. Rea (Oxford, UK: Oxford University Press, 2009), 271.

[70] Ibid., 270.

[71] *Compendium Theologica* Q227; trans. accessed at http://dhspriory.org/thomas/Compendium.htm#227.

[72] Ibid.

[73] Luther, *Large Catechism*, Part 2: Article II; trans. accessed at http://www.ccel.org/ccel/luther/largecatechism.iii_2.html.

substitutionary death.[74] While Luther appealed to Anselm's theory of satisfaction, Arnold notes that he went beyond Anselm in stressing the anger of God against sin and subsequently Jesus as he bore the sins of humanity on the cross.[75] Arnold also notes that Luther, along with the Latin tradition, also affirmed the early Greek ecclesiastical tradition of Christ's triumph over the powers of this world.[76]

Luther's main stress, though, was the substitutionary nature of Christ's death. Christ died for us and for our sin. For Luther, Christ was innocent and yet humbled himself to be obedient to death in order that our sins might be forgiven. Commenting on Galatians 3:13, Luther famously noted:

> Thus the whole emphasis is on the phrase "for us." For Christ is innocent so far as His own Person is concerned; and therefore He should not have been hanged from the tree. But because, according to the Law, every thief should have been hanged, therefore, according to the Law of Moses, Christ Himself should have been hanged; for he bore the person of a sinner and a thief — and not of one but of all sinners and thieves. . . . In short, He has and bears all the sins of all men in His body — not in the sense that He has committed them, but in the sense that He took these sins, committed by us, upon His own body, in order to make satisfaction for them with His own blood.[77]

Luther's stress here captures the leading view of the doctrine during the Reformation and also proves to have a lasting influence on further theological discourse.

John Calvin

Calvin, after affirming the central tenets of the creeds concerning the facts of Jesus,[78] further developed the theme of substitution highlighted by Luther in order to further answer why Jesus had to die on the cross for the sins of humanity. Calvin viewed the incarnation, death, and resurrection as central to the story of redemption, but he also noted that Scripture ascribed special significance to the passion and death of Christ.[79]

---

[74] Matthieu Arnold, "Luther on Christ's Person and Work," in *The Oxford Handbook of Martin Luther's Theology*, eds. Robert Kolb, Irene Dingel, and Lubomir Batka (Oxford, UK: Oxford University Press, 2014), 283.

[75] Ibid., 284.

[76] Ibid.

[77] *Lectures on Galatians*; trans. *Luther's Works*, vol. 26, 277.

[78] See *Institutes* II.14.5.

[79] Ibid., II.16.5; here Calvin cites Matt 10:28; Rom 3:25, 4:25, 5:9; John 1:29; 2 Cor 5:21.

He affirmed that Apostles' Creed underscores this by connecting Christ's birth with his suffering and death. He wrote, "In the Confession of Faith, called the Apostles' Creed, the transition is admirably made from the birth of Christ to his death and resurrection, in which the completion of a perfect salvation consists."[80] In regard to substitution he emphatically stressed, "Our acquittal is in this that the guilt which made us liable to punishment was transferred to the head of the Son of God (Isa 53:12)."[81]

Jaesung Cha notes that the seeds of substitution theory seen in Augustine, Anselm, and Aquinas come to fruition with Calvin, who stressed the legal nature of the transaction as well as the wrath of God.[82] Cha further notes, "This substitutionary punishment, which Christ bears, is viewed by Calvin as appeasement of God's wrath."[83] Paul Van Buren notes that Calvin viewed the creedal statements of Christ's burial and descent into hell as a part of his substitutionary work in that he represented humanity even into the grave.[84] Like Luther, Calvin's developed doctrine of the atonement greatly influenced the theological discourse after him and continues to have a lasting voice in conversation.

Karl Barth

As noted in the previous two case studies, Barth's own theological development was greatly guided and informed by the creedal proclamations of the church. Within that framework, he then sought to explore the implications of such proclamations. For Barth, dogmatic theology focused on assessing and proclaiming the truth of the message of the church.[85] Concerning the passion of Jesus, Barth saw it as an "unveiling of man's rebellion and of God's wrath, yet also of His mercy."[86] In affirming the factual statements of the creeds concerning Christ's incarnation, death, and resurrection, Barth also sought to understand the depth of the event.

In agreement with Luther[87] and Calvin, Barth stressed substitution as a key theme of the doctrine. Remarking on the humiliation and exaltation

---

[80] *Institutes* II.16.5

[81] Ibid.

[82] Jaeseung Cha, "Calvin's Concept of Penal Substitution," in *Restoration through Redemption: John Calvin Revisited*, ed. H. Van Den Belt (Leiden, Netherlands: Brill, 2013), 114.

[83] Ibid.; cf. *Institutes* II.16.2.

[84] Paul Van Buren, *Christ in Our Place* (Grand Rapids, MI: Eerdmans, 1957), 56; cf. *Institutes* II.16.8.

[85] Barth, *Dogmatics in Outline*, 5.

[86] Ibid., 109.

[87] Barth noted that, in substance, Luther's understanding of Gal 3:13 was "quite right." See *Church Dogmatics* 4/1, trans. Geoffrey W. Bromiley and Thomas F. Torrance (Edinburgh, Scotland: T & T Clark, 1962), 238.

of Christ, he noted, "The picture before us is that of an inconceivable exchange, of a *katalage*, that is, a substitution. Man's reconciliation with God takes place through God's putting Himself in man's place and man's being put in God's place, as a sheer act of grace. It is this inconceivable miracle which is our reconciliation."[88]

Barth notes that the simple yet powerful phrase, *for us*, contains this great truth of substitution, and that "whatever a doctrine of reconciliation tries to express, it *must* say this."[89] For Barth, this substitution means that the punishment for sin has been rendered to Christ and therefore no longer falls on humanity. Free of this curse, humanity can now be righteous in God's sight.[90]

Barth was quick to note, though, that no single theory of the great mystery of the atonement can exhaustively express the range and depth of the action. For Barth, all theories of the atonement are only "pointers," highlighting one aspect of the truth contained in the great event.[91] He viewed the *theologia gloriae* of the Eastern Church as a complement to the Western and Lutheran *theologia crucis*.[92] Adam Johnson notes that Barth's approach to the doctrine embraces "the unified diversity of Jesus' saving work."[93]

Karl Rahner

As the previous two case studies have shown, Rahner sought to explore the open area within but beyond the creedal proclamations of the church. The themes drawn out by the great voices of the church preceding Rahner serve as guides as well as critical dialogue partners. Rahner was very critical of Anselm's theory of satisfaction, fearing that it misrepresented the justice of God and could too easily be included in ransom-to-Satan theories.[94]

George Vass notes that, for Rahner, Christology and soteriology are inseparably connected.[95] One cannot understand the work of Christ without understanding the person, and the person of Christ informs the work of

---

[88] *Dogmatics in Outline*, 115.

[89] Ibid., 116.

[90] *Credo*, 93.

[91] *Dogmatics in Outline*, 116.

[92] Ibid., 114.

[93] Adam J. Johnson, *God's Being in Reconciliation: The Theological Basis of the Unity and Diversity of the Atonement in the Theology of Karl Barth* (London: T & T Clark, 2012), 198.

[94] Rahner, *Foundations of Christian Faith*, 289–90. Rahner also noted in this section that calling attention to the limits of traditional dogmatic statements is not the same as contradicting them. George Vass notes that Rahner does not completely abandon the Anselmian theory only extends beyond it. See George Vass, *Understanding Karl Rahner* (Westminster, MD: Christian Classics U.a., 1985), 7.

[95] Vass, *Understanding Karl Rahner*, 1.

Christ. Instead of satisfaction or substitution, Rahner prefers to view the work of Christ as a mediation of God's salvific will. Rahner wrote:

> The pure initiative of God's salvific will establishes the life of Jesus which reaches fulfillment in his death, and hence this salvific will becomes manifest as irrevocable. The life and death of Jesus taken together, then, are the "cause" of God's salvific will . . . insofar as the life and death of Jesus, or the death which recapitulates and culminates his life, possess a causality of a quasi-sacramental and real-symbolic nature.[96]

Vass notes that, for Rahner, the death of Jesus stands as the permanent mediation of God's will to save his people.[97] Rahner stressed here that God's will to save and Christ's death on the cross are correlated causes of the process of redemption. It is not only Christ's blood that makes reconciliation possible but also the fact that God desired humanity to be saved. Rahner attempted to replace the vengeful God of classic theories with a God who seeks to provide a way of salvation out of love and grace, a God who wills to save.

Vass sums up Rahner's "theory of atonement" as consisting of two parts: (1) God's salvific will as an *a priori* cause, and (2) the incarnation, death, and resurrection of Christ as a mediating cause.[98] Rahner affirmed that the creeds and New Testament regard the death of Jesus as the cause of atonement, but he also sought to identify the precise causal nature of the act.[99]

While Rahner pushed the conversation to uncomfortable limits, he is included here not as an endorsement of his view but as an example of deeper theological investigation that also respects essential identity markers articulated in the proclamations of the church. The freedom of his investigation is attested by the wide area left unexplored by the classic creedal proclamations.

Implications for Teaching the Doctrine Today

The lack of a formal ecclesial-endorsed theory of the atonement has provided fertile ground for further theological inquiry and speculation. The inquiry has not been left without critical guides, however. Key voices over the preceding two millennia of the church have identified and articulated several basic themes of the Christian narrative concerning the atonement:

---

[96] Rahner, *Foundations*, 284.
[97] Vass, *Understanding Karl Rahner*, 4.
[98] Ibid., 14–15.
[99] Rahner, *Foundations*, 282.

sacrifice, satisfaction, substitution, propitiation, expiation, and triumph, to list a few. These themes can at times appear in conflict with one another, and each taken in isolation fails to capture the complexity and diversity of the biblical narrative. The student of theology can easily become overwhelmed by the myriad of theories concerning the atonement. The EIM approach to theology seeks to provide biblically grounded guides to aid in navigating and assessing the various theories.

As one navigates the myriad of theories concerning the atonement, it is important to recognize and affirm (and in many ways reaffirm) crucial themes that emerge from the biblical narrative that were noted by the church. In regard to the atonement, several key themes emerged that can be noted as essential to Christian identity. An examination of two of these themes will highlight their functions as essential identity markers and relevant guides in navigating further theological investigation.

The first crucial theme that emerges from the biblical narrative was summed up in the creeds as the simple phrase *for us*. Barth stressed this in his own understanding of the doctrine, as noted above.[100] This simple phrase captures the themes of ransom, satisfaction, substitution, and sacrifice. The concept that the Christ event was for us is so evident in the biblical narrative that whatever else one notes about the event, one must include this concept.

The second crucial theme that emerges from the biblical narrative is that through the cross and resurrection of Jesus Christ, God utterly defeated the powers of sin, death, and darkness. The biblical narrative is clear that Jesus emerges as the triumphant savior.[101] This is the foundation of the Christus Victor view of the atonement. Death no longer has the final word, and sin no longer has power over its captives. The death and resurrection of Jesus display God's power over the powers and principalities of the world. The church proclaimed this message of triumph as a message of hope. There is peace for the battle is won. Much like the concept *for us*, Christ as victor is vitally important in understanding the implications of the doctrine. Presently, this view is the preferred view in global theological discourse. The wrathful God of substitutionary views has been eclipsed by a victorious God.

In isolation, though, neither of these identity markers tells the complete story. Here one must understand the Barthian idea that the various theories of the atonement serve as "pointers" not ends in themselves.[102] They reflect an aspect of the theological prism. The two identity markers referenced here serve as guides in navigating new waters of theological thought. The teacher of theology would do well to clearly identify and

---

[100] Barth, *Dogmatics in Outline*, 116.
[101] See Heb 2:14; 1 John 3:8; Gal 1:4, 4:3; Col 1:12.
[102] Barth, *Dogmatics in Outline*, 5.

articulate these EIMs in order to provide these guides for the student lost in a sea of conflicting voices.

The teacher would also do well in noting that, while one theory may appear to capture a larger picture of the doctrine they all point to a much more complex picture of God's salvific action. Bird describes the various theories of the atonement as spokes on a wheel.[103] While all the spokes connect to the wheel, one theory may more fully capture the complexity of the doctrine and best be described as the hub. In noting the importance of all theories, Bird also validates placing more emphasis on one theory over the others.[104]

The doctrine of the atonement highlights the complex nature of theological discourse and the need for clear markers to guide the conversation. One isolated view, even if drawn from Scripture, is not sufficient in capturing the magnitude of the doctrine. One isolated view, without the complement of the other views proclaimed in the biblical narrative, can also lead the theological community to paint a one-dimensional picture of God that fails to tell the complete story at best and depicts a wildly different God at worst. The EIM model seeks to identity and articulate all relevant primary affirmations of the biblical narrative and to construct a doctrinal stance that takes each affirmation into account. Without the recognition of all clear markers, the theological discourse concerning the atonement will remain fractured and combative.

---

[103] Bird, *What Christians Ought to Believe*, 132.

[104] Ibid. For Bird, the victory of theory serves as an "integrative model for the atonement since it effectively combines the motifs of recapitulation, representation, ransom, sacrifice, and triumph."

5

Implications for Teaching Theology Using the EIM Model

Almost two thousand years have passed since the life, death, and resurrection of Jesus Christ. Over these millennia a multitude of voices have joined the chorus of Christian theology. These voices have ranged from simple affirmations of the unique Christian identity presented in Scripture to far deeper investigations of theological mysteries. We now stand at a time in history when the many voices of theology fluctuate between harmony and dissonance. Assessing the nuances of each voice and grasping the bigger picture of Christian theology can be a difficult task for the church and students of theology.

During its first three centuries, the church faced similar theological uncertainties. To help navigate the varying theological voices, the church identified primary affirmations of the biblical narrative which served to assess the various theological assertions being made at the time as well as guide further theological exploration. These primary affirmations took shape in the form of creedal proclamations. The creedal proclamations, in turn, became summaries of the core beliefs that gave shape to a unique Christian identity.

Today, probing deeper into uncharted theological territories while affirming the tested traditions of the church can be a difficult task. This book has proposed an approach to theology to help the church and the student of theology navigate this sea of voices and strike a proper balance between tradition and exploration. This approach, the EIM model, is shaped by the creedal process of the first three centuries of the church. This concluding chapter will first note the influence of the creedal process on the EIM model and detail how the EIM model serves as a mirror of the creedal process. It will then highlight six implications of teaching theology via the creedal process using the EIM model. Three objections to using the EIM model will also be examined in order to answer key concerns one might have in using the model.

EIM Model as Mirror of the Creedal Process

In proposing the EIM model as an effective approach to systematic theology, this book has used the creedal process as a guide. Early Christian creedal formulations, those appearing in both the Hebrew Bible and the New Testament, up to the later fourth-century formulations, provide certain key characteristics of the creedal process. A primary objective of early creedal formulations was to succinctly articulate the essential affirmations of the Christian faith. Yoder noted these affirmations as "fence-posts" that clearly defined the basic tenets of the faith.[1] Kelly considered them summaries of "the essential articles" of the Christian faith.[2]

These affirmations served to define the unique Christian identity revealed in the biblical narrative and further explored by the church. These essential affirmations were then used to assess other theological statements. Emerging theological statements which rejected or negated these affirmations were deemed to lie outside of the fence posts of traditional Christian proclamation.

Another objective of the creedal process was the passing on of tradition, or *paradosis*. Paul clearly noted this as he set up the early creedal formulation in 1 Cor 15, which was examined in both chapters two and five. Here Paul highlighted his passing on to the Christians in Corinth the tradition he had received. The tradition referenced in 1 Cor 15 is a short summary of the death and resurrection of Jesus Christ. This creedal formulation provided the church with an easy method for spreading the core narrative of the gospel. Augustine asserted that the creedal formulations of the church were used to teach new converts essential beliefs in a way that they could easily understand and memorize.[3]

As summaries of the essential articles of the Christian faith, these early creedal formulations were not meant to be exhaustive or cover each category of theology. As noted in the previous chapter, Anselm observed the incomplete nature of the creeds and asserted that they were not intended to be an exhaustive list of all Christian belief but rather a starting place.[4] This incomplete nature of creedal formulations highlights their proper functions of structuring and facilitating further theological discourse. The EIM model seeks to mirror this aspect of creedal process and apply it to the various categories of theology.

By mirroring the creedal process, the EIM model seeks to clearly re-identify and re-articulate the essential identity markers of the Christian faith. As defined in chapter one, essential identity markers are primary

---

[1] Yoder, *Preface to Theology*, 223.
[2] Kelly, *Early Christian Creeds*, 1.
[3] Augustine, *Retractions* I.1.
[4] Anselm, *On the Procession of the Holy Spirit* 13.

affirmations of the biblical narrative. These identity markers are labeled *essential* when without them, theological statements lose their unique Christian identity. Therefore, EIMs are primary affirmations that make Christian theology uniquely Christian. While the biblical narrative serves as the primary source for identifying EIMs, it is also important to note how these EIMs have been recognized and articulated by the church. In this way, tradition sheds light on the church's understanding of these distinct EIMs. Tradition also helps underscore the essential nature of each marker.

For example, the first case study on the creedal development of Trinitarian and Christological thought noted several key EIMs that guided the theological discourse of the first three centuries of the church. The first EIM discussed was the proclamation that "God is one." One sees this proclamation in both the Hebrew Bible and the New Testament, from the Shema to the letters of Paul.[5] One also sees Jesus Christ proclaimed and worshiped as God, serving as another EIM of the biblical narrative. These two EIMs, among others regarding the topic, served to guide the theological discourse of the early church fathers.[6] This discourse led to the formulation of succinct statements and confessions that articulated both the divinity of Christ and the triune nature of God.

The second case study focused on the creedal development of the doctrine of Creation. This case study stressed that an overwhelming proclamation of the biblical narrative is that God is the creator of heaven and earth. This primary affirmation can be drawn out of every section of Scripture, from the first lines of the book of Genesis to the sermons of Paul in the book of Acts. It served as a ground for worship in the book of Psalms and a distinguishing characteristic of God among other gods in the biblical period. In terms of a unique Christian identity it is clearly an essential affirmation, and to deny it is to step outside of Christian theology. This essential identity marker drawn from the biblical narrative grounded the great creeds of the early church and continues to serve as a guide in navigating the intersection of faith and science in twenty-first-century theology.

The third case study, covering the development of the doctrine of the Atonement, stood out as a vivid example of the benefits of the EIM model. While no single formally endorsed proclamation of the church has defined how Christ's death on the cross wrought atonement for sin, certain primary affirmations of the biblical narrative serve as necessary guides in formulating a more complete understanding of the doctrine. The biblical narrative clearly affirms that Christ's death was in some way *for* the sins of

---

[5] See Deut 6:4–5; Isa 45:5–6; 1 Cor 8:6; and 1 Tim 2:5.

[6] Here is where Lindbeck would note them as "regulative principles." See *Nature of Doctrine*, 80–81.

humanity.[7] The biblical narrative also affirms that Christ's death and resurrection signaled his victory over the powers and principalities of this world.[8] Theories of the Atonement that have been developed over the millennia of Christian theology often tend to highlight one of these EIMs over the other. Describing both as essential ensures a balanced tone in further theological discourse.

These case studies served to exemplify the key characteristics and benefits of the EIM model. One key characteristic of the model is that it focuses primarily on answering questions of *who* and *what*. Who is the God of the Christian faith? What is God like? What are essential elements of God's identity presented in the biblical narrative? What has God done? The EIM model is less concerned with directly answering questions of *how*. How does the Trinity work together in unity and distinction? How did God create? How does Christ's death on the cross atone for the sins of humankind? In reference to the doctrine of biblical inspiration, I. Howard Marshall wrote, "The doctrine of inspiration is a declaration that the Scriptures have their origin in God; it is not and cannot be an explanation of *how* God brought them into being."[9]

How questions are not ignored though. They represent the open space defined by the EIMs and long to be explored. The greater work of theology is to explore these deeper questions. The key of the EIM model, meanwhile, is to clearly have in mind the essential affirmations of the biblical narrative before embarking on deeper theological exploration.

The survey of the creedal process in chapter two made it clear that theological development was not intended to end with the early church fathers and the creedal formulations of the church during their time. As Barth stressed, the church must "again and again" attempt to understand the creedal formulations of the past.[10] The EIM model approach to theology seeks to identify and articulate the essential identity markers of the biblical narrative for a new generation, who, like all generations according to Barth, must approach theology afresh again and again.

Implications for Teaching Theology via the EIM Model

The EIM model of theology is not the only viable approach to theology but it is a timely approach that will aid a new generation's further exploration of the fundamental affirmations of the Christian faith. As this book concludes, it will be important to explore several implications and benefits of utilizing

---

[7] See 1 Cor 15:3–4; Gal 3:13; 1 Pet 2:21.

[8] See Heb 2:14; 1 John 3:8; Gal 1:4, 4:3; Col 1:12.

[9] I. Howard. Marshall, *Biblical Inspiration* (Grand Rapids, MI: Eerdmans Pub., 1983), 44. Emphasis mine.

[10] Barth, *Credo*, 4.

the EIM model. First, the EIM model fulfills the core functions of theology by articulating essential identity markers and reflecting on their deeper implications. Second, with this interplay between articulation and reflection, the EIM model provides objectivity with freedom. Third, this model guards against theological agnosticism, which has grown in light of the numerous theological voices as well as modern and postmodern epistemological concerns. Fourth, the EIM model fosters ecumenical unity. Fifth, the EIM model appeals to the shifting cultural landscape of postmodernity. And last, the EIM approach to theology provides a better way for the church to assess cultural influence on theology.

Articulation and Reflection

Definitions of *theology* are numerous. Etymologically, the term refers to the study of God, but the discipline of theology is much more complex than this simple definition, for even this simple definition is more complex than it appears. Barth describes theology as a "free science."[11] It is a science in that it is a discipline of study and discovery, and yet it is fundamentally different in regard to the relationship between the student and the object of study.

According to Barth, "Theology is a free science because it is based on and determined by the kingly freedom of the word of God," the object of study.[12] The theologian does not have control over his object of study the way a biological scientist does while examining the dissected remains of a cadaver. For Barth, theology as a free science is the act of relating humanity to God, not of relating God to humanity. God, as the object of study, is free and inexhaustible and cannot be brought down to the level of humanity. Since God is a free object of study, God's freedom also frees the theologian from any "dependence on subordinate presuppositions."[13]

Millard Erickson defines theology as a "discipline that strives to give a coherent statement of the doctrines of the Christian faith, based primarily on the Scriptures, placed in the context of culture in general, worded in a contemporary idiom, and related to issues of life."[14] With this definition Erickson highlights the doctrinal nature of theology while also noting the importance of cultural context. Similarly, David Clark notes that "theology seeks to articulate the content of the gospel of Jesus Christ to the context of a particular culture."[15] Stanley Grenz defines theology as the

---

[11] Barth, *Evangelical Theology*, 9. See also *Dogmatics in Outline*, 5.

[12] *Dogmatics in Outline*, 5.

[13] *Evangelical Theology*, 9.

[14] Erickson, *Christian Theology*, 28.

[15] David K. Clark *To Know and Love God: Method for Theology* (Wheaton, IL: Crossway Books, 2003), 1.

"systematic reflection on, and articulation of, the fundamental beliefs we share as followers of Jesus Christ."[16]

It is clear from these definitions that a core function of theology is the articulation of fundamental affirmations of the Christian faith. Another core function of theology drawn out in other definitions is the function of reflection. Daniel Migliore stresses that "theology must be a *critical reflection* on the beliefs and practices of the faith community out of which it arises. Theology is not simply a reiteration of what has been or is currently believed and practiced by a community of faith."[17] McGrath notes that theology is "both the process of reflecting on the Bible and weaving together its ideas and themes."[18] Grenz and Franke define theology as:

> An ongoing, second-order, contextual discipline that engages in critical and constructive reflection on the faith, life, and practices of the Christian community. Its task is the articulation of biblically normed, historically informed, and culturally relevant models of the Christian belief-mosaic for the purpose of assisting the community of Christ's followers in their vocation to live as the people of God in the particular social-historical context in which they are situated.[19]

Theology is not simply the articulation of fundamental beliefs, for after they were articulated, there would be no further need for theology. Theology must include reflection and investigation. As Migliore stresses, theology is much more than just repeating the beliefs of past generations or, one could add, creedal formulations. Along with articulation, theology is also a discipline of reflection.

In mirroring the creedal process, the EIM model best performs both functions of theology. The primary function of the EIM model is the articulation of primary affirmations of the biblical narrative. This articulation guides the theological conversation into greater reflection and investigation. As seen in the above definitions, proper theology requires both. If theology is only articulation, then the conversation is cut short. If theology is only reflection it becomes too ethereal and enigmatic. Theology, then, offers no real answers and loses its influence in the real world,

---

[16] Stanley J. Grenz, *Created for Community: Connecting Christian Belief with Christian Living* (Grand Rapids, MI: Baker Books, 1998), 15.

[17] Migliore, *Faith Seeking Understanding*, 9.

[18] Alister E. McGrath, *Theology: The Basics* (Malden, MA: Blackwell Pub., 2004), 1.

[19] Stanley J. Grenz and John R. Franke, *Beyond Foundationalism: Shaping Theology in a Postmodern Context* (Louisville, KY: Westminster John Knox Press, 2001), 16.

remaining primarily a thought experiment for theologians. Theology needs both the substance of articulation and the freedom of reflection.

Objectivity with Freedom

Another implication of employing the EIM model in teaching theology is that it offers objectivity with freedom. The grand conversation of theology is neither unguided nor purely subjective. One can know certain core affirmations of the biblical narrative that have been recognized and proclaimed by the church. One can proclaim them again for new generations as they examine and reflect on the proclamations of the past. Objectivity grounds the process of reflection and removes the fear of exploring new ideas. By holding onto essential identity markers, one need not fear getting it "wrong" theologically. Without this fear, one is truly free to explore deeper mysteries and take more chances.

Tertullian, writing about the essential identity markers summarized in the Rule of Faith, stated, "Provided the essence of the Rule is not disturbed, you may seek and discuss as much as you like. You may give full rein to your itching curiosity where any point seems unsettled and ambiguous or dark and obscure."[20] Tertullian stressed here that once the essential affirmations are known and guarded, one has immense freedom in exploring deeper matters. One does not need to be timid in this exploration either, but rather can give "full rein" to curiosity.

While exploring the procession of the Holy Spirit in light of the biblical narrative and earlier developed Trinitarian thought, Anselm also acknowledges the freedom one has to explore, as long as the core tenets of the faith are held. For Anselm, the core tenets are summarized by the early creeds and if one does not proclaim something that is contrary to the proclamations of the creeds, one is safe.[21]

On the other hand, freedom is a necessary part of the theological process because it allows each new generation to ask their own unique questions and seek relevant answers. Theological freedom also allows for differences of interpretation. Augustine notes this need for freedom and objectivity in light of interpretation when writing about his own interpretation of a biblical psalm. He notes, "Some other person may produce a better interpretation, for the obscurity of the scriptures is such that a passage scarcely ever yields a single meaning only. But, whatever interpretation emerges, it must conform to the rule of faith."[22] When this

---

[20] Tertullian, *Prescriptions Against Heretics* 14; trans. Greenslade, *Early Latin Theology*, 40.

[21] *On the Procession of the Holy Spirit* 13.

[22] Augustine, *Expositions of the Psalms* 74.12; trans. by Maria Boulding, *Expositions of the Psalms* (New York: New City Press, 2000), 4:50.

principle is applied to theological discourse, voices are allowed the freedom to differ amongst themselves as long as they do not contradict the essential identity markers.

Theological Agnosticism

Along with providing objectivity with freedom, the creedal process of identifying and articulating the essential identity markers of Christian theology also guards against the subtle yet pervasive spread of theological agnosticism. Theological agnosticism, here, refers to the idea that the many contradictory voices within Christian theology denote a lack of certain knowledge in the realm of theology. The student of theology may note that Augustine claimed one thing while Aquinas another. Luther stressed a certain aspect of salvation by grace while his contemporaries stressed another. Wesley disagreed with Calvin and so on and so forth. This can, then, lead the student of theology to question what one can actually *know* theologically. Often the student is left feeling that theology is primarily a subjective discipline.

The subjective nature of theology was a hallmark of the theological approach of Schleiermacher. For him, theology was not grounded in historical facts, morals, or even metaphysics, but rather the experience of the divine common to each individual. Alexander Bruce notes that for Schleiermacher, theology is "not the science of God as he is in himself, but the knowledge of God as he affects us through the world and through Christ, or the knowledge of our own mental states as thus affected."[23] Bruce goes on to note that underlying Schleiermacher's approach, and later Ritschl's, is the fundamental belief in the severe limitation of theological knowledge.[24] One cannot truly know God but only how one experiences God. Schleiermacher's approach, though thoroughly disputed by Barth and others, continues to influence new, more increasingly postmodern generations.

In contrast, the EIM model seeks to highlight what is known about God as revealed in the biblical narrative and passed down through tradition. It serves to stress that certain affirmations about God can be recognized as capturing the essential identity of Christian theology. These fundamental affirmations then guide and shape the rest of theology. This theological knowledge is not affected by contradictory voices or subjective experience.

The EIM model does not teach, however, that one is capable of exhaustively knowing God. By focusing on the essential identity markers, this approach also affirms that there is plenty that is not known about God and much that never will be known. Here the balance between the

---

[23] Alexander Balmain Bruce, "Theological Agnosticism," *The American Journal of Theology* 1, no. 1 (1897): 2.
[24] Ibid., 3–4.

knowability of God and the incomprehensibility of God is carefully kept. The EIM model seeks to teach the student of theology that one can know something about God while also encouraging further exploration of the unknown.

Ecumenical Unity

By focusing on the essentials, the EIM model also provides a foundation for greater ecumenical unity. The desire for unity among the diverse churches of the first three centuries of Christianity served as a primary impetus for early creedal formulations. The unifying nature of creedal formulations can be particularly seen in the writings of Paul. Often when Paul refers to an earlier creedal formulation, he does so to note a unity of belief between himself and the church or person he is writing to.

In the opening lines of the book of Romans, as Paul introduces himself to a church to which he is has not traveled, he references a brief creedal statement that serves as the core of the gospel of Jesus (Rom 1:3–4).[25] While the origin and authorship of the creedal statement is debated, it is clear that Paul references key essential identity markers of the Christian faith that both he and the church in Rome hold. In this shared belief Paul establishes unity with the Romans before he proceeds with his letter. In his letter to the Philippians Paul also uses an earlier creedal formulation to remind the church of her core beliefs and establish unity within the church (Phil 2:5–11).

The later conciliar creeds also provided a foundation for greater ecumenical unity. As summaries of the core beliefs of the Christian faith, they unified the developing and evolving church around a core narrative. It should be noted here that the unity provided by the conciliar creedal formulations was not a forced unity. John Meyendorff notes that the creed formulated at the Council of Nicaea did not create unity but rather symbolized the unity of the church concerning shared beliefs.[26]

The *filioque* controversy does highlight the limitations of the unity provided by formal creedal formulations. It should be stressed though that the controversy concerns a single phrase inserted into the creed without full confirmation. The controversy does not reflect the creedal process or the unifying nature of creedal formulations as a whole. Meyendorff goes on to stress that correctly understood the Nicene Creed is "not only one of the

---

[25] See James D. G. Dunn, *Romans 1–8* (WBC 38A; Dallas, TX: Word, 1988), 5, for a discussion on the creedal nature of the phrasing in the two verses.

[26] Meyendorff, "The Nicene Creed: Uniting or Dividing Confession," 15.

uniting factors of past ecclesiastical history, it is the most traditionally authoritative expression of the Christian faith."[27]

The unifying nature of the EIM model is evident when it is applied to different categories of theology. For example, the third case study noted incongruences surrounding the various theories of the doctrine of the Atonement. Often those who hold strongly to one theory of the Atonement conflict with those holding another view. The EIM model seeks to provide a common ground for all sides of the conversation surrounding any given doctrine. While some disagree on the precise nature of the Atonement, they can find unity in what is affirmed by the EIMs. This unity should also provide cause for charity toward those who hold opposing views noting that essential beliefs are affirmed. As noted with the doctrine of the Atonement, the EIM model helps shed light on the complex nature of certain doctrines and provides the adequate grounds for diversity within unity.

Shifting Cultural Landscape of Postmodernity

Writing about theological method within a postmodern context, Grenz and Franke note two import aspects of the postmodern ethos: "the fundamental critique and rejection of modernity, and the attempt to live and think in a realm of chastened rationality characterized by the demise of modern epistemological foundationalism."[28]

While it is not within the scope of this work to critique Grenz and Franke's conclusion as it pertains to theology within a postmodern context, it is important for us to note that theology is currently undertaken in sharply different cultural context than in previous generations. As Grenz and Franke note, the epistemological certainty of modernity has been rejected, along with its dualism and assumption of the goodness of knowledge and progress.[29] Theology can no longer rest on the cherished tenets of modernism. For Grenz and Franke, theology must be viewed in a more constructivist and communitarian light.

The EIM model of theology, while not forgoing foundational, universal truth claims, acknowledges the role of the Christian community in reflecting on the theological proclamations of the church. The EIM model acknowledges the vast uncertainty of theological knowledge while at the same time providing normative guides which aid the community of faith in its fresh exploration of deeper questions of theology. As noted in previous chapters of this study, the early creedal formulations also support and encourage further theological exploration. The sheer brevity of the early formulations provides immense space for theological reflection.

---

[27] Meyendorff, "The Nicene Creed: Uniting or Dividing Confession," 19.

[28] Grenz and Franke, *Beyond Foundationalism*, 19.

[29] Ibid., 21–22.

In regard to the doctrine of creation, this study observed, in agreement with Samuel Powell, that the early creedal formulations affirm actually very little other than that God is the creator.[30] This limited yet fundamental affirmation leaves sufficient room for new communities of faith to explore its overarching implications. It can also be noted that the early creedal formulations were themselves constructed in community. They were products of communal reflection and theological investigation of the core of the biblical narrative.

Assessment of Advancement and Cultural Influence

It has been clearly noted in this study, especially in the survey of varying definitions of theology above, that theology is a contextual discipline. Theology does not happen in a vacuum but rather is shaped by its particular cultural context. The cultural context of the fourth century and the growth of alternative expressions of Christianity led to the formation of the conciliar creeds. The culture of the church in the sixteenth century led to the Reformation, and so on.

Justo González notes that "knowledge of Christ never comes to us apart from culture, or devoid of cultural baggage."[31] Without the proper identity markers it can be difficult to gauge whether the advancements within theology due to cultural influence are beneficial, though. Establishing clear essential identity markers which remain stable in the flux of cultural tides, provides a way of assessing theological advancement and the influence of culture.

Claude Welch, surveying Protestant thought of the nineteenth century, notes a critical distinction between liberal and conservative thought. Welch notes that liberal theology can be characterized by a "maximum acknowledgement of the claims of modern thought."[32] Conversely, conservative theology can be characterized by a maximum acknowledgement of the claims of traditional thought. The EIM model seeks to understand a middle ground between these two poles where the claims of modern thought are assessed by the stable features of traditional thought and traditional thought is further interpreted in light of modern claims.

This assessment is clearly needed in matters of scientific advancement and theology. As noted in the second case study, modern claims of human origins must be measured and guided by the overwhelming proclamation of the biblical narrative of God as creator of heaven and earth.

---

[30] Powell, *Participating in God*, 8.

[31] Justo L. González, *Out of Every Tribe and Nation: Christian Theology at the Ethnic Roundtable* (Nashville, TN: Abingdon Press, 1992), 30.

[32] Claude Welch, *Protestant Thought in the Nineteenth Century*, vol. I (New Haven, CT: Yale University Press, 1972), 142.

Yet, in areas where there is no clear identity marker there is freedom to explore the implications of modern advancements. The EIM model notes that not all claims of modern thought can or should be accepted without modification, and neither are all the claims of traditional thought so fixed that new insight cannot shape greater understanding of certain doctrines.

Objections to Creedal Theology and the EIM Model

The six implications of teaching theology within the creedal framework via the EIM model listed above have stressed the benefits of using this model especially in the current theological climate. It will be helpful, though, to also examine a few potential objections to theology within a creedal framework and the EIM model.

The first objection that could be leveled against using the EIM model would be the notion that even the EIMs themselves are debatable and insufficient grounds for building a theological framework. This objection also calls into question the method with which the EIMs are established. Given the debatable nature of many theological claims this appears to be a valid concern. The key to responding to this objection is to understand the limited nature of the EIMs. EIMs are not intended to be numerous nor to cover each area of the doctrine they are guiding. The creedal process provides an excellent model for this. The claims made by the Apostles' and Nicene Creeds are not numerous or exhaustive. They are focused on the core of the biblical narrative as it pertains to the unique identity of the God of Christianity. As confessions became longer and more denominationally specific, they ventured further into the areas marked off by the EIMs of the earlier creeds.

The key for the EIM model will be to clearly delineate between EIMs themselves and further theological speculations grounded in the EIMs. Another key will be to keep the EIMs limited in number and reserved for only those claims that enjoy overwhelming biblical support. Following the creedal process of identifying and articulating only the most essential identity markers will be critical in moving the EIMs beyond debate. This does not mean, though, that the EIMs are beyond interpretation. EIMs are identified so that their theological meaning may be debated and explored by the community of faith.

A second objection that could be raised against creedal theology and the EIM model is that creedal formulations and EIMs elevate church tradition too highly and threaten the authority of Scripture. Michael Bird notes this objection in his work on creedal theology. Bird notes that in certain evangelical circles there is a definite anticreedal strain which cautions against placing church tradition over Scripture.[33] Bird stresses, though, the biblical nature of the creedal process itself, citing several protocreedal formulations in both the Old and New Testaments.

The biblical foundation sections of the three case studies examined in this study also serve to highlight the biblical nature of the EIMs as well. Neither early creedal formulations nor EIMs are the creations of church tradition alone. The central foundation for each is the biblical narrative. It is true that the councils and theological minds of the church helped in identifying them, but their source is and must be the biblical narrative. Establishing strong biblical support for each EIM is critical in assuaging this objection. Also, the limited number of true EIMs will aid in underscoring their overwhelming biblical support.

A third objection that can be raised against the EIM model is that it only focuses on a small portion of theology. This study has described theology as a grand conversation. It can also be described as palatial mansion with many rooms and hidden doorways. To some, the EIM model may seem like only exposing people to the front entryway but nothing further. If EIMs, or the creeds themselves for that matter, were designed to stop the conversation this objection would be more valid.

As stressed in this study, early creedal formulations and EIMs are not intended to provide the final answers of theology but rather to guide and shape the ongoing conversation. In the analogy of a palatial mansion, the EIMs would function more like walls than gates. These walls provide strength and structure for the house but there are many rooms in which to explore. It is important to note that the EIM model of theology is not a comprehensive systematic theology, but rather a way of approaching theology that provides the proper space for the community of faith to further explore.

Concluding Remarks

Theology is a grand conversation, comprised of a myriad of voices and viewpoints. A great temptation exists within theology today, however, which could signal the loss of a unique Christian identity. It is the temptation of absolute freedom. This age holds a desire to free theology, and the world, from the shackles of dogmatic, creedal tradition. This desire comes from both secular and conservative sides, albeit for different reasons, and is often accompanied by a severe distrust of tradition. Yet it appears that a grave misunderstanding of the creedal process and the true function of the creeds also accompanies this desire.

---

[33] Bird, *What Christians Ought to Believe*, 18.

As noted earlier, the creedal formulations of the early church were never meant to serve as shackles constricting further theological exploration. They were, and still are, relevant guides in assessing the crowded conversation of theology. Early creedal formulations identified and articulated primary affirmations of the biblical narrative not to put an end to the conversation but rather to focus the conversation on the unique Christian identity of God as presented in Scripture. Dissenting voices were not condemned simply because they were different but because they failed to affirm essential elements of the Christian story. They were simply not Christian. The creedal process of the first three centuries of the church exhibits theology's need for these clear, narratological markers.

The EIM model constructed and proposed in this book offers an approach to theology that mirrors the creedal process and seeks to identify and articulate the essential identity markers relevant to each different category of theology. These EIMs then guide the conversation as the community of faith seeks to explore the space framed by these markers. Theology is truly free in this sense, free to explore the implications of the EIMs in new and provocative ways, and free from stepping outside the narrative of Scripture.

The EIMs are greatly needed to retain the essential elements of Christian theology as each new generation of the church seeks to understand its beliefs and proclaim the message of Christianity again and again. As Barth stressed, the church must understand its core confession so that it can confess it anew to new and changing generations.[34] Creedal theology and the EIM model seek to guide the grand theological discourse of the church in faithful articulation and honest reflection of the core narrative of the Christian faith. In light of the EIM model, the church can engage in the grand theological conversation with confidence and freedom.

---

[34] Barth, *Credo*, 4.

Bibliography

Althaus, Paul. *The Theology of Martin Luther*. Translated by Robert Schultz. Philadelphia: Fortress Press, 1966.

Ambrose. *Letter 42*.

Anselm. *On the Procession of the Holy Spirit*.

Aquinas, Thomas. *Compendium Theologica*.

———. *De Potentia*.

———. *Expositio in Symbolum Apostolorum*.

———. *Summa Theologica*.

Arand, Charles P. "Luther on the Creed." *Lutheran Quarterly* 20, no. 1 (2006): 1–25.

Ashwin-Siejkowski, Piotr. *The Apostles' Creed: The Apostles' Creed and Its Early Christian Context*. London: T & T Clark, 2009.

Athanasius. *On the Incarnation of the Word*.

Augustine. *Against the Manicheans*.

———. *Contra Faustum Manichaeum*.

———. *De Trinitate*.

———. *Expositions of the Psalms*. Translated by Maria Boulding. Vol. 4. New York: New City Press, 2000.

———. *On Faith and the Creed*.

———. *On the Holy Trinity*.

———. *Retractions*.

Ayres, Lewis. *Augustine and the Trinity*. Cambridge, UK: Cambridge University Press, 2010.

———. "Augustine on the Rule of Faith: Rhetoric, Christology, and the Foundation of Christian Thinking." *Augustinian Studies* 36, no. 1 (2005): 33–49.

Badcock, F. J. *The History of the Creeds*. New York: Macmillan, 1930.

Barth, Karl. *Church Dogmatics*. Translated by Geoffrey W. Bromiley and Thomas F. Torrance. Edinburgh: T & T Clark, 1962.

———. *Credo*. New York: Charles Scribner's Sons, 1962.

———. *Dogmatics in Outline*. Translated by G. T. Thomson. New York: Harper & Row, 1959.

———. *Evangelical Theology: An Introduction*. New York: Holt, Rinehart and Winston, 1963.

———. *The Faith of the Church: A Commentary on the Apostles' Creed According to Calvin's Catechism*. New York: Meridian Books, 1958.

Basil. *The Hexaemeron*.

Bates, Matthew W. *The Birth of the Trinity: Jesus, God, and Spirit in New Testament and Early Christian Interpretations of the Old Testament*.

Bauckham, Richard. *Jesus and the God of Israel: God Crucified and Other Studies on the New Testament's Christology of Divine Identity*. Grand Rapids, MI: Eerdmans, 2009.

———. "Paul's Christology of Divine Identity." Reading, Annual Meeting of the Society of Biblical Literature, Toronto, November 25, 2002. http://www.foranswer.org/Top_JW/Ricahrd_Bauckham.pdf.

Baur, Ferdinand Christian, Peter Crafts Hodgson, and Robert F. Brown. *History of Christian Dogma*.

Beatrice, Pier Franco. "The Word "Homoousios" from Hellenism to Christianity." *Church History* 71, no. 02 (2002): 243. doi:10.1017/s0009640700095688.

Behr, John. *Irenaeus of Lyons: Identifying Christianity*. Oxford: Oxford University Press, 2013.

———. *The Way to Nicaea*. Vol. 1. The Formation of Christian Theology. Crestwood, NY: St. Vladimir's Seminary Press, 2001.

Belt, H. Van Den, ed. *Restoration through Redemption: John Calvin Revisited*. Leiden: Brill, 2013.

Bird, Michael F. *What Christians Ought to Believe: An Introduction to Christian Doctrine through the Apostles' Creed*. Kindle ed. Grand Rapids: Zondervan, 2016.

Blaising, Craig A. "Creedal Development as Hermeneutical Development: A Reexamination of Nicaea." *Pro Ecclesia* XIX, no. 4 (2010): 371–88.

Blowers, Paul M. "Beauty, Tragedy and New Creation: Theology and Contemplation in Cappadocian Cosmology." *International Journal of Systematic Theology* 18, no. 1 (2016): 7–29.

Blowers, Paul M. *Drama of the Divine Economy: Creator and Creation in Early Christian Theology and Piety*. Oxford: Oxford University Press, 2012.

Boethius. *On the Catholic Faith*.

Bouteneff, Peter. *Beginnings: Ancient Christian Readings of the Biblical Creation Narratives*. Grand Rapids, MI: Baker Academic, 2008.

Boyarin, Daniel. "The Gospel of the Memra: Jewish Binitarianism and the Prologue of John." *Harvard Theological Review* 94 (2001): 243–84.

Brümmer, Vincent. *Atonement, Christology and the Trinity: Making Sense of Christian Doctrine*. Aldershot, England: Ashgate, 2005.

Bruce, Alexander Balmain. "Theological Agnosticism." *The American Journal of Theology* 1, no. 1 (1897): 1–15.

Buren, Paul Van. *Christ in Our Place*. Grand Rapids: Eerdmans, 1957.

Burnaby, Hugh. *Thinking through the Creed; Addresses in a College Chapel*. London: Hodder and Stoughton, 1961.

Burnaby, John. *The Belief of Christendom: A Commentary on the Nicene Creed*. London: SPCK, 1960.

Calvin, John. *Institutes of the Christian Religion*.

Childs, Brevard S. *Biblical Theology of the Old and New Testaments: Theological Reflection on the Christian Bible*. Minneapolis: Fortress Press, 1993.

Clark, David K. *To Know and Love God: Method for Theology*. Wheaton, IL: Crossway Books, 2003.

Clark, Gordon Haddon. *Karl Barth's Theological Method*. Philadelphia: Presbyterian and Reformed Pub., 1963.

Clark, Mary T. "De Trinitate." *The Cambridge Companion to Augustine*: 91–102.

Clement of Rome. *1 Clement*.

Cullmann, Oscar. *The Earliest Christian Confessions*. London: Lutterworth Press, 1949.

Davies, Brian, and Brian Leftow, eds. *The Cambridge Companion to Anselm*. Cambridge, UK: Cambridge University Press, 2004.

Davies, Brian. *The Thought of Thomas Aquinas*. Oxford: Clarendon Press, 1992.

Donovan, Mary Ann. *One Right Reading?: A Guide to Irenaeus*. Collegeville, MN: Liturgical Press, 1997.

Dunn, James D. G. *Romans 1–8*. WBC. Dallas: Word, 1988.

Dünzl, Franz. *A Brief History of the Doctrine of the Trinity in the Early Church*. London: T & T Clark, 2007.

Emery, Gilles, and Francesca Aran. Murphy. *The Trinitarian Theology of Saint Thomas Aquinas*. Oxford: Oxford University Press, 2007.

Ensor, Peter. "Tertullian and Penal Substitutionary Atonement." *Evangelical Quarterly* 82, no. 2 (2014): 130–42.

Erickson, Millard J. *Christian Theology*. Grand Rapids, MI: Baker Book House, 1998.

Fairbairn, Donald. *Life in the Trinity: An Introduction to Theology with the Help of the Church Fathers*. Downers Grove, IL: IVP Academic, 2009.

Fairweather, William. *Origen and Greek Patristic Theology*. New York: Scribner, 1901.

Fee, Gordon D. "Philippians 2:5–11: Hymn or Exalted Pauline Prose?" *Bulletin for Biblical Research* 2 (1992): 29–46.

Ferguson, Everett. "Tertullian." *The Expository Times* 120, no. 7 (2009): 313–21. doi:10.1177/0014524609103464.

———. *The Rule of Faith: A Guide*. Eugene, OR: Cascade Books, 2015.

Fitzgerald, Allan, and John C. Cavadini, eds. *Augustine through the Ages: An Encyclopedia*. Grand Rapids, MI: W.B. Eerdmans, 1999.

Fuhrmann, Paul T. *An Introduction to the Great Creeds of the Church*. Philadelphia: Westminster Press, 1960.

Gibson, Edgar C. S. *The Three Creeds*. London: Longmans, Green &, 1912.

González, Justo L. *A History of Christian Thought*. Rev ed. Vol. I. Nashville: Abingdon Press, 1993.

———. *Out of Every Tribe and Nation: Christian Theology at the Ethnic Roundtable*. Nashville: Abingdon Press, 1992.

Goodspeed, Edgar J., and Robert M. Grant. *A History of Early Christian Literature*. Chicago: University of Chicago Press, 1966.

Green, Joel B., and Mark D. Baker. *Recovering the Scandal of the Cross: Atonement in New Testament & Contemporary Contexts*. Downers Grove, IL: InterVarsity Press, 2000.

Greenslade, S. L., ed. *Early Latin Theology: Selections from Tertullian, Cyprian, Ambrose, and Jerome*. Philadelphia: Wes..ninster Press, 1978.

Gregory of Nazianzus. *Oration 45*.

Gregory of Nyssa. *Greater Catechism*.

Grensted, L. W. *A Short History of the Atonement*. Manchester: Manchester University Press, 1920.

Grenz, Stanley J., and John R. Franke. *Beyond Foundationalism: Shaping Theology in a Postmodern Context*. Louisville, KY: Westminster John Knox Press, 2001.

Grenz, Stanley J. *Created for Community: Connecting Christian Belief with Christian Living*. Grand Rapids, MI: Baker Books, 1998.

Grudem, Wayne A. *Systematic Theology: An Introduction to Biblical Doctrine*. Leicester, England: Inter-Varsity Press, 1994.

Harnack, Adolf Von. *The Apostles' Creed*. Translated by Stewart Means. Edited by T. Bailey Saunders. London: A. and C. Black, 1901.

Hartog, Paul, ed. *The Contemporary Church and the Early Church: Case Studies in Ressourcement*. Kindle ed. Eugene: Pickwick, 2010.

———. *Orthodoxy and Heresy in Early Christian Contexts: Reconsidering the Bauer Thesis*. Eugene: Pickwick, 2015.

———. "The 'Rule of Faith' and Patristic Biblical Exegesis." *Trinity Journal* 28, no. 1 (Spring 2007): 65–86.

Heim, S. Mark, ed. *Faith to Creed: Ecumenical Perspectives on the Affirmation of the Apostolic Faith in the Fourth Century: Papers of the Faith to Creed Consultation, Commission on Faith and Order, NCCCUSA, October 25–27, 1989--Waltham, Massachusetts*. Grand Rapids, MI: W.B. Eerdmans for Commission on Faith and Order, National Council of the Churches of Christ in the U.S.A., 1991.

Henry, Martin. "Karl Barth on Creation." *Irish Theological Quarterly* 69, no. 3 (2004): 219–23.

Holmes, Stephen R. *The Quest for the Trinity: The Doctrine of God in Scripture, History, and Modernity*. Downers Grove, IL: IVP Academic, 2012.

Holsinger-Friesen, Thomas. *Irenaeus and Genesis: A Study of Competition in Early Christian Hermeneutics*. Winona Lake, IN: Eisenbrauns, 2009.

Horton, Michael Scott. *The Christian Faith: A Systematic Theology for Pilgrims on the Way*. Grand Rapids, MI: Zondervan, 2011.

———. *We Believe: Recovering the Essentials of the Apostles' Creed*. Nashville, TN: Word Pub., 1998.

Ignatius of Antioch. *Epistle to the Smyrneans*.

———. *Epistle to the Trallians*.

Ip, Pui Him. "Re-imagining Divine Simplicity in Trinitarian Theology." *International Journal of Systematic Theology* 18, no. 3 (2016): 274–89.

Irenaeus. *Against Heresies*.

———. *Demonstration of Apostolic Preaching*.

Jenson, Robert W. *Canon and Creed*. Interpretation: Resources for Use of Scripture in the Church. Louisville, KY: Westminster John Knox Press, 2010.

Johnson, Adam J. *God's Being in Reconciliation: The Theological Basis of the Unity and Diversity of the Atonement in the Theology of Karl Barth*. London: T & T Clark, 2012.

Johnson, Luke Timothy. *The Creed: What Christians Believe and Why It Matters*. New York: Doubleday, 2003.

Jowers, Dennis W. *The Trinitarian Axiom of Karl Rahner: The Economic Trinity Is the Immanent Trinity and Vice Versa*. Lewiston, NY: Edwin Mellen Press, 2006.

Kelly, J. N. D. *Early Christian Creeds*. 2nd ed. New York: D. McKay, 1961.

———. *Early Christian Doctrines*. New York: Harper, 1959.

Kolb, Robert, Irene Dingel, and Lubomir Batka, eds. *The Oxford Handbook of Martin Luther's Theology*. Oxford: Oxford University Press, 2014.

Kooi, Cornelis Van Der. "Calvin's Theology of Creation and Providence: God's Care and Human Fragility." *International Journal of Systematic Theology* 18, no. 1 (2016): 47–65.

La Due, William J. *The Trinity Guide to the Trinity*. Harrisburg, PA: Trinity Press International, 2003.

Leith, John H. *Creeds of the Churches: A Reader in Christian Doctrine, from the Bible to the Present*. 3rd ed. Atlanta: John Knox Press, 1982.

Lewis, C. S. *The Problem of Pain*. New York, NY: HarperOne, 2001.

Lindbeck, George A. *The Nature of Doctrine: Religion and Theology in a Postliberal Age*. Philadelphia: Westminster Press, 2009.

Litfin, Bryan M. "Learning from Patristic Use of the Rule of Faith." In *The Contemporary Church and the Early Church: Case Studies in Ressourcement*, edited by Paul Hartog, Kindle Edition. Eugene: Pickwick, 2010.

———. *Getting to Know the Church Fathers: An Evangelical Introduction*. Grand Rapids, MI: Brazos Press, 2007.

Lohse, Bernhard. *A Short History of Christian Doctrine*. Philadelphia: Fortress Press, 1966.

Lonergan, Bernard J. F. *Method in Theology*. New York: Herder and Herder, 1972.

Longenecker, Richard N. *New Wine into Fresh Wineskins: Contextualizing the Early Christian Confessions*. Peabody, MA: Hendrickson Publishers, 1999.

Luther, Martin. *Large Catechism*.

———. *Lectures on Galatians*.

———. *The Magnificant*.

———. *Small Catechism.*

Macleod, Donald. *Christ Crucified: Understanding the Atonement*. Downers Grove, IL: InterVarsity Press, 2014.

Mann, William E. "Anselm on the Trinity." In *The Cambridge Companion to Anselm*, edited by Brian Davies and Brian Leftow. Cambridge, UK: Cambridge University Press, 2004.

Marshall, I. Howard. *Biblical Inspiration*. Grand Rapids, MI: Eerdmans Pub., 1983.

Marthaler, Berard L. *The Creed: The Apostolic Faith in Contemporary Theology*. Mystic, CT: Twenty-Third Publications, 1987.

Martyr, Justin. *Apology.*

———. *Dialogue with Trypho.*

Maspero, Giulio, and Robert J. Wozniak, eds. *Rethinking Trinitarian Theology: Disputed Questions and Contemporary Issues in Trinitarian Theology*. London: T & T Clark, 2012.

McCormack, Bruce L., and Kimlyn J. Bender, eds. *Theology as Conversation: The Significance of Dialogue in Historical and Contemporary Theology: A Festschrift for Daniel L. Migliore*. Grand Rapids, MI: William B. Eerdmans Pub., 2009.

McGiffert, Arthur Cushman. *The Apostles' Creed: Its Origin, Its Purpose, and Its Historical Interpretation*. New York: C. Scribner's, 1902.

Mcgowan, Andrew Brian. "Tertullian and the 'Heretical' Origins of the 'Orthodox' Trinity." *Journal of Early Christian Studies* 14, no. 4 (Winter 2006): 437–57.

McGrath, Alister E. *Christian Theology: An Introduction*. Third ed. Oxford, UK: Blackwell Publishers, 2001.

———. *I Believe: Understanding and Applying the Apostles' Creed*. Grand Rapids, MI: Zondervan, 1991.

———. *Theology: The Basics*. Malden, MA: Blackwell Pub., 2004.

Meyendorff, John. "The Nicene Creed: Uniting or Dividing Confession." In *Faith to Creed: Ecumenical Perspectives on the Affirmation of the Apostolic Faith in the Fourth Century: Papers of the Faith to Creed Consultation, Commission on Faith and Order, NCCCUSA, October 25–27, 1989--Waltham, Massachusetts*, edited by S. Mark Heim. Grand Rapids, MI: W.B. Eerdmans for Commission on Faith and Order, National Council of the Churches of Christ in the U.S.A., 1991.

Migliore, Daniel L. *Faith Seeking Understanding: An Introduction to Christian Theology*. Grand Rapids: W.B. Eerdmans, 1991.

Migne, Jacques Paul. *Patrologiae Cursus Completus: Sive Bibliotheca Universalis, Integra, Omnium Ss. Patrum, Doctorum, Scriptorumque Ecclesiasticorum, Sive Latinorum, Sive Graecorum*. Translated by Adalbert Hamman. Paris: Garnier, 1960.

Neufeld, Vernon H. *The Earliest Christian Confessions*. Grand Rapids: Eerdmans, 1963.

O'Donovan, Leo J. *A World of Grace: An Introduction to the Themes and Foundations of Karl Rahner's Theology*. New York: Seabury Press, 1980.

Oliver, Simon. "Augustine on Creation, Providence and Motion." *International Journal of Systematic Theology* 18, no. 4 (2016): 379–98.

Olson, Roger E. *The Story of Christian Theology: Twenty Centuries of Tradition & Reform*. Downers Grove, IL: InterVarsity Press, 1999.

Origen. *Homilies in Numbers*.

———. *In Ioh.*

———. *In Matthew.*

———. *In Romans.*

———. *On First Principles.*

Osborn, Eric Francis. *Irenaeus of Lyons*. Cambridge: Cambridge University Press, 2001.

Packer, J. I. *Affirming the Apostles' Creed*. Wheaton, IL: Crossway Books, 2008.

Papandrea, James L. *The Earliest Christologies: Five Images of Christ in the Postapostolic Age*. Downers Grove, IL: IVP Academic, 2016.

Pelikan, Jaroslav. *The Christian Tradition: A History of the Development of Doctrine: The Emergence of the Catholic Tradition, 100–600*. Vol. 1. Chicago: University of Chicago Press, 1971.

———. *Credo: Historical and Theological Guide to Creeds and Confessions of Faith in the Christian Tradition*. New Haven, CT: Yale University Press, 2003.

Polycarp. *Epistle to the Philippians*.

Powell, Samuel M. *Participating in God: Creation and Trinity*. Minneapolis: Fortress Press, 2003.

Prestige, G. L. *God in Patristic Thought*. Translated by F. L. Cross. London: S.P.C.K., 1952.

Rahner, Karl. *Foundations of Christian Faith: An Introduction to the Idea of Christianity*. Translated by William V. Dych. New York: Crossroads, 1996.

———. *Hominisation; the Evolutionary Origin of Man as a Theological Problem*. New York: Herder and Herder, 1965.

———. *Theological Investigations*. Vol. 1. Baltimore: Helicon Press, 1965.

———. *The Trinity*. New York: Burnes & Oates, 2001.

Reynolds, Stephen M. "[Calvin's View of the Athanasian and Nicene Creeds." *Westminster Theological Journal* 23, no. 1 (November 1960): 33–37.

Richardson, Alan. *Creeds in the Making: A Short Introduction to the History of Christian Doctrine*. Philadelphia: Fortress Press, 1981.

Rombs, Ronnie J., and Alexander Y. Hwang, eds. *Tradition & the Rule of Faith in the Early Church: Essays in Honor of Joseph T. Lienhard, S.J.* Washington, D.C.: Catholic University of America Press, 2010.

Schaff, Philip. *The Creeds of Christendom: With a History and Critical Notes*. Vol. I. Grand Rapids: Baker Books, 1996.

Schleiermacher, Friedrich. *The Christian Faith*. Edited by Paul T. Nimmo. New York: Bloomsbury T. & T. Clark, 2016.

Soskice, Janet. "Aquinas and Augustine on Creation and God as 'Eternal Being.'" *New Blackfriars* 95, no. 1056 (2014): 190–207.

Stauffer, Ethelbert. *New Testament Theology*. Translated by John Marsh. New York: Macmillan, 1956.

Steenberg, Irenaeus M. C. *Irenaeus on Creation: The Cosmic Christ and the Saga of Redemption*. Leiden: Brill, 2008.

Stump, Eleonore. "Atonement According to Aquinas." In *Oxford Readings in Philosophical Theology. Volume 1, Trinity, Incarnation, and Atonement*, edited by Michael C. Rea. Oxford: Oxford University Press, 2009.

Tertullian. *Against Hermogenes*.

———. *Against Marcion*.

———. *Against Praxeas*.

———. *On Modesty*.

———. *Prescriptions Against Heretics*.

Thiselton, Anthony C. *The First Epistle to the Corinthians: A Commentary on the Greek Text*. NIGTC. Grand Rapids, MI: W.B. Eerdmans, 2000.

Thom, Paul. *The Logic of the Trinity: Augustine to Ockham*. New York: Fordham University Press, 2012.

Thomas, and John Fearon. *Summa Theologiae*. London: Blackfriars., 1969.

Trueman, Carl R. *The Creedal Imperative*. Wheaton, IL: Crossway, 2012.

Turner, C. H. *The History and Use of Creeds and Anathemas in the Early Centuries of the Church*. 2nd ed. London: Society for Promoting Christian Knowledge, 1910.

Vass, George. *Understanding Karl Rahner*. Westminster, MD: Christian Classics U.a., 1985.

Walton, John H. *Genesis*. NIV Application Commentary. Grand Rapids, Mich: Zondervan, 2001.

Welch, Claude. *Protestant Thought in the Nineteenth Century*. Vol. I. New Haven: Yale University Press, 1972.

Wendel, Francóis. *Calvin: The Origins and Development of His Religious Thought*. Translated by Philip Mairet. New York: Harper & Row, 1963.

Westra, Liuwe H. *The Apostles' Creed: Origin, History, and Some Early Commentaries*. Turnhout, Belgium: Brepols, 2002.

Wilken, Robert Louis. *The Spirit of Early Christian Thought: Seeking the Face of God*. New Haven: Yale University Press, 2003.

Wingren, Gustaf. *Man and the Incarnation: A Study in the Biblical Theology of Irenaeus*. Philadelphia: Muhlenberg Press, 1959.

Yarnell, Malcolm B. *The Formation of Christian Doctrine*. Nashville, TN: B & H Academic, 2007.

Yoder, John Howard. *Preface to Theology: Christology and Theological Method*. Grand Rapids, MI: Brazos Press, 2002.

Young, Frances M. *The Making of the Creeds*. London: SCM Press, 1991.

Zachman, Randall C. *John Calvin as Teacher, Pastor, and Theologian: The Shape of His Writings and Thought*. Grand Rapids, MI: Baker Academic, 2006.

Zizioulas, John D. *Lectures in Christian Dogmatics*. Edited by Douglas H. Knight. London: T & T Clark, 2008.

———. "The Doctrine of the Holy Trinity: The Significance of the Cappadocian Contribution." In *Trinitarian Theology Today: Essays on Divine Being and Act*, edited by Christoph Schwöbel. Edinburgh: T & T Clark, 1995.

CPSIA information can be obtained
at www.ICGtesting.com
Printed in the USA
BVHW091702301120
594467BV00012B/495